Living Wisdom from the World's Religions

Living Wisdom

FROM THE

World's
Religions

365 Daily Readings of Insight and Inspiration

EDITED BY GEORGE L. ABERNETHY

Holt, Rinehart and Winston · New York Chicago San Francisco

Acknowledgments

Grateful acknowledgment is made to the following for their kind permission to include selections from the books listed:

George Allen & Unwin Ltd., London, for excerpts from *The Faith and Practice of Al-Ghazali*, translated by W. Montgomery Watt (1953); for passages from *Rumi: Poet and Mystic*, edited by R. A. Nicholson (1950); and for excerpts from *The Koran Interpreted*, translated by Arthur J. Arberry (1955).

Allenson & Co. Ltd., London, for selections from *An Indian Peasant Mystic*, edited by John S. Hoyland (1932).

Association Press, YMCA Publishing House, Calcutta, India, for excerpts from *Psalms of Maratha Saints*, translated by Nicol Macnicol (1920).

The Buddhist Society, London, for excerpts from *Tao-Te-Ching*, translated by Ch'u Ta-Kao (1937).

Cambridge University Press for selections from *The Jataka or Stories of the Buddha's Former Births*, translated by W. H. D. Rouse (1895).

Bruno Cassirer (Publishers) Ltd., Oxford, for excerpts from *Buddhist Texts Through the Ages*, edited by Edward Conze (1954).

The Clarendon Press, Oxford, for excerpts from *The Sikh Religion* by M. A. Macauliffe (1909); and for extracts from *The Heart of Buddhism*, edited by K. J. Saunders (1915).

E. P. Dutton & Co., Inc., New York, and J. M. Dent & Sons Ltd., London, for excerpts from *Chinese Philosophy in Classical Times*, edited, annotated, and translated by E. R. Hughes, Everyman's Library (1942).

Fortune Magazine and Reinhold Niebuhr for a passage from "A Faith for History's Greatest Crisis," by Reinhold Niebuhr, *Fortune*, Vol. XXVI, No. 1 (July 1942).

Harper & Row, Publishers, Inc., for selections from *Introduction to the Devout Life* by St. Francis de Sales, edited and translated by John K. Ryan (1950).

Harvard University Press and the Loeb Classical Library for a passage from *Epictetus: The Discourses as Reported by Arrian, The Manual and Fragments*, translated by W. A. Oldfather (1928).

Horizon Press for selections from *Hasidism and Modern Man* by Martin Buber, copyright 1958.

Raphael Loewe, and the World Publishing Co. for selections from *A Rabbinic Anthology*, edited by C. G. Montefiore and H. Loewe (originally published by Macmillan & Co., Ltd., London, 1938).

Luzac & Company, Ltd., London, for a passage from *Psalms of a Saiva Saint*, translated by T. Isaac Tambyah (1925).

For Bob and Jean

Preface

THE Wisdom Literature of the Hebrews as it appears in Proverbs, Job, Ecclesiastes, and other books is well known. These writings are international and cosmopolitan rather than exclusively Hebraic in character. They are paralleled in other cultures and religions. They still speak to us across the ages with liveliness and relevance. The insights presented here are in turn shrewd, pithy, penetrating, practical, ironic, critical, sensitive, appreciative, and speculative observations of life. Although this traditional Wisdom Literature is well represented in this volume, I have not limited my selections to it. I have included many selections which are "wisdom" in a much looser and broader sense. I have tried to maintain some balance between familiar and unfamiliar material, between difficult and simple selections.

Although the choices represent some personal interest, it is hoped that each selection will be found to contain something worthy of brief meditation during any reader's busy day. No claim is made that any selection can be fully understood out of the context from which it has been torn. The only claim is that it possesses sufficient intrinsic interest and merit to bear thoughtful meditation. Thus this diary of daily readings is not an attempt to provide a synthesis or common denominator for the truth to be found in the various world religions. It is simply a testimony to the conviction that today our personal needs are so great that no possible source of truth, goodness, inspiration, or reflection should be dismissed without thoughtful examination.

Sources and Bibliography will be found at the end of the book.

Davidson, North Carolina   G. L. A.

Living Wisdom from the World's Religions

Of God's Companionship

You cannot do better than so arrange your time as to read a short time every day, with some brief meditation, reviewing your weak points, considering your duties, seeking God, and acquiring the habit of familiar intercourse with him. Happy will you be if you learn what it is to find love an occupation. It is no use to ask what those who love God do with him. There is no difficulty in spending our time with a friend we love; our heart is always ready to open to him; we do not study what we shall say to him, but it comes forth without premeditation; we can keep nothing back—even if we have nothing special to say, we like to be with him. Oh, how much easier it is to love than to fear! Fear constrains, fetters, perplexes one; but love persuades, comforts, inspirits, expands the soul, and makes one desire what is good for its own sake. It is true that one always needs a fear of the judgment of God as a counterpoise to the passions. "My flesh trembleth for fear of Thee." May my whole body be filled with thy fear, O Lord. But if we begin with a fear which subdues the flesh, we must reach on to that love which comforts the soul. How good and faithful a friend you will find in God, if you will but form a sincere, steadfast friendship with him!

FRANÇOIS DE FÉNELON

The Parable of Me and Mine

Some children were playing beside a river. They made castles of sand, and each child defended his castle and said, "This one is mine." They kept their castles separate and would not allow any mistakes about which was whose. When the castles were all finished, one child kicked over someone else's castle and completely destroyed it. The owner of the castle flew into a rage, pulled the other child's hair, struck him with his fist and bawled out, "He has spoilt my castle! Come along all of you and help me to punish him as he deserves." The others all came to his help. They beat the child with a stick and then stamped on him as he lay on the ground. . . . Then they went on playing in their sand-castles, each saying, "This is mine, no one else may have it. Keep away! Don't touch my castle!" But evening came; it was getting dark and they all thought they ought to be going home. No one now cared what became of his castle. One child stamped on his, another pushed his over with both his hands. Then they turned away and went back, each to his home.

YOGACARA BHUMI SUTRA

DAY 3   HINDUISM

The Nearness of Death

Do good today, time passes, Death is near.
Death falls upon a man all unawares,
Like a ferocious wolf upon a sheep.
Death comes when his approach is least expected.
Death sometimes seizes ere the work of life
Is finished, or its purposes accomplished.
Death carries off the weak and strong alike,
The brave and timorous, the wise and foolish,
And those whose objects are not yet achieved.
Therefore do not delay; Death may come today.
Death will not wait to see if you are ready,
Or if your work is done. Be active now,
While you are young, and time is still your own.
This very day perform tomorrow's work,
This very morning do your evening's task.
When duty is discharged, then if you live,
Honor and happiness will be your lot,
And if you die, supreme beatitude.

MAHABHARATA

The Superior Man

Tsze-kung asked what constituted the superior man. The Master said, "He acts before he speaks, and afterwards speaks according to his actions.

"The superior man is catholic and no partisan. The mean man is a partisan and not catholic. A scholar, whose mind is set on truth, and who is ashamed of bad clothes and bad food, is not fit to be discoursed with. The superior man, in the world, does not set his mind either for any thing, or against any thing; what is right he will follow. The superior man thinks of virtue; the small man thinks of comfort. The superior man thinks of the sanctions of law; the small man thinks of favors which he may receive. He who acts with a constant view to his own advantage will be much murmured against. A man should say, I am not concerned that I have no place, I am concerned how I may fit myself for one. I am not concerned that I am not known, I seek to be worthy to be known."

The Master said of Tsze-ch'an that he had four of the characteristics of a superior man: in his conduct of himself, he was humble; in serving his superiors, he was respectful; in nourishing the people, he was kind; in ordering the people, he was just.

ANALECTS

The Land

In the Name of God, the Merciful, the Compassionate

No! I swear by this land,
and thou art a lodger in this land;
by the begetter, and that he begot,
indeed, We created man in trouble.
What, does he think none has power over him,
saying, "I have consumed wealth abundant"?
What, does he think none has seen him?

Have We not appointed to him two eyes,
and a tongue, and two lips,
and guided him on the two highways?
Yet he has not assaulted the steep;
and what shall teach thee what is the steep?
The freeing of a slave,
or giving food upon a day of hunger
to an orphan near of kin
or a needy man in misery;
then that he become of those who believe
and counsel each other to be steadfast,
and counsel each other to be merciful.

Those are the Companions of the Right Hand.
And those who disbelieve in Our signs,
they are the Companions of the Left Hand;
over them is a Fire covered down.

THE KORAN

DAY 6   TAOISM

The Child From God

When the men of Kuo fled, one of them, named Lin Hui, cast aside most valuable regalia and carried away his child upon his back. Someone suggested that he was influenced by the value of the child—but the child's value was small. Or by the inconvenience of the regalia—but the inconvenience of the child would be much greater. Why then did he leave behind the regalia and carry off the child?

Lin Hui himself said, "The regalia involved a mere question of money. The child was from God."

And so it is that in trouble and calamity mere money questions are neglected, while we ever cling nearer to that which is from God. And between neglecting and clinging to, the difference is great.

CHUANG TZU

The Works and Work of God

The heavens declare the glory of God; and the firmament sheweth his handiwork. Day unto day uttereth speech, and night unto night sheweth knowledge. There is no speech nor language, where their voice is not heard. Their line is gone out through all the earth, and their words to the end of the world. In them hath he set a tabernacle for the sun. Which is as a bridegroom coming out of his chamber, and rejoiceth as a strong man to run a race. His going forth is from the end of the heaven, and his circuit unto the ends of it: and there is nothing hid from the heat thereof. The law of the Lord is perfect, converting the soul: the testimony of the Lord is sure, making wise the simple. The statutes of the Lord are right, rejoicing the heart: the commandment of the Lord is pure, enlightening the eyes. The fear of the Lord is clean, enduring for ever: the judgments of the Lord are true and righteous altogether. More to be desired are they than gold, yea, than much fine gold: sweeter also than honey and the honeycomb. Moreover, by them is thy servant warned; and in keeping of them there is great reward. Who can understand his errors? cleanse thou me from secret faults. Keep back thy servant also from presumptuous sins; let them not have dominion over me: then shall I be upright, and I shall be innocent from the great transgression. Let the words of my mouth, and the meditation of my heart, be acceptable in thy sight, O Lord, my strength, and my redeemer.

PSALM 19

Love of Neighbor

The man who truly loves his neighbor therefore loves also his enemy. This distinction, "friend or enemy," is a difference in the object of love, but love for one's neighbor truly has an object which is without discrimination; the neighbor is the absolutely in-distinguishable difference between man and man, or it is the eternal resemblance before God—and the enemy also has this resemblance. We think that it is impossible for a man to love his enemy, alas! for enemies can hardly bear to look at each other. Oh, well, then close your eyes—then the enemy absolutely re-sembles your neighbor; close your eyes and remember the com-mandment that *thou shalt love,* then you love—your enemy? No, then you love your neighbor, for you do not see that he is your enemy. That is, if you close your eyes, then you do not see the earthly difference; but enmity is also one of the earthly differences. And when you close your eyes, then your mind is not distracted and diverted at the very moment when you should listen to the word of the commandment. Then when your mind is not dis-tracted and diverted by looking at the object of your love and at the difference in the object, then you become merely an ear for hearing the word of the commandment which said to you, and to you alone, that "thou" shalt love thy neighbor. Lo, then are you on the way of perfection toward loving your neighbor, when your eye is closed and you are become only an ear for hearing the com-mandment.

SØREN KIERKEGAARD, Works of Love

DAY 9   HINDUISM

The World's Illusion

Entangled in a hundred worldly snares,
Self-seeking men, by ignorance deluded,
Strive by unrighteous means to pile up riches.
Then, in their self-complacency, they say,
"This acquisition I have made today,
That I will gain tomorrow; so much wealth
Is hoarded up already, so much more
Remains that I have yet to treasure up.
This enemy I have also destroyed, him also
And others in their turn I will dispatch.
I am a lord; I will enjoy myself;

I'm wealthy, noble, strong, successful, happy;
I'm absolutely perfect; no one else
In all the world can be compared to me.
Now I will offer up a sacrifice,
Give gifts with lavish hand and be triumphant."
Such men, befooled by endless, vain conceits,
Caught in the meshes of the world's illusion,
Immersed in sensuality, descend
Down to the foulest hell of unclean spirits.

BHAGAVAD-GITA

DAY 10   JUDAISM
The Judgment of Wrongdoers

When Rabbi Bunam was a young man, a friend borrowed a few dollars from the chest established for the repairing of damaged synagogue books in order to donate a gift to a poor man who was collecting funds for the marriage dowries of dowerless brides. This became known and the trustees summoned the borrower to a hearing. The defendant asked Rabbi Bunam to serve as his counsel.

Rabbi Bunam narrated the following well-known fable: "There was once an epidemic among the animals of the forest. The lion, the tiger, the wolf and the fox held a consultation, and the fox affirmed his belief that the epidemic was due to a great sin committed by some resident of the forest. He advised that all the animals assemble and confess their transgressions. The beasts of prey first confessed, and their excuses were accepted. Finally a sheep timidly approached and confessed that she had eaten a little hay from her owner's mattress.

" 'Aha,' roared the lion, 'you are the great sinner. You have abused your master's confidence.' And the sheep was condemned to death."

Rabbi Bunam then turned to the judges, and said, "You, Reb Leo, have been guilty of this and this; and you, Reb Bear, have done so and so; you, Reb Wolf, have acted wrongly in this and this instance. Yet you dare sit in judgment against a kind-hearted

9

man because he has borrowed money for a highly worthy cause."

Everyone present felt ashamed and left without pronouncing judgment against the defendant.

NIFLAOTH RABBI BUNAM

The Bracelets

There was a king of Benares. One summer when the weather was very hot he lay down in an upper room on a couch adorned with gold, silver and many precious stones, and made a servant massage him with ointment of sandalwood from the Bull's Head Mountain. The servant was wearing a great many bracelets on her arms, and they jangled together while she massaged the king. The sound irritated him and he asked her to take one of the bracelets off. She did so, and there was a little less noise. She took off another, and there was less noise still. He made her go on taking them off till there was only one left, and then there was no jangling at all. When the noise stopped the king had a sudden awakening. "That is just what I ought to do with my kingdom, my ministers, subjects, concubines and attendants," he said to himself. "In fact, with all business and bother." From that moment onward he had no further worldly desires, but spent his time meditating in complete seclusion, and became a Solitary (Pratyeka) Buddha.

TSO-CH'AN SAN-MEI CHING

Justice and Kindness

Someone said, "What do you say concerning the principle that injury should be recompensed with kindness?"

The Master said, "With what then will you recompense kindness? Recompense injury with justice, and recompense kindness with kindness."

The Master said, "Alas! there is no one that knows me."

Tsze-kung said, "What do you mean by thus saying that no one knows you?" The Master replied, "I do not murmur against Heaven. I do not grumble against men. My studies lie low, and my penetration rises high. But there is Heaven; that knows me!"

Yuen Jang was squatting on his heels, and so waited the approach of the Master, who said to him, "In youth, not humble as befits a junior; in manhood, doing nothing worthy of being handed down; and living on to old age—this is to be a pest." With this he hit him on the shank with his staff.

ANALECTS

DAY 13   ISLAM
The Being of Man Is Like a Forest

The being of man is like a forest; be full of caution of this being if you are of that breath. In our being there are thousands of wolves and hogs. In our being there is the righteous, the unrighteous, the fair and the foul.

That trait which is predominant decides the temperament: when gold exceeds copper in quantity, the substance is gold. The quality which is predominant in your being—you will have to rise in the very form of that same quality.

At one moment wolfishness comes into man; at another moment, the moon-like beauty of the face of Joseph. Feelings of peace and of enmity go by a hidden road from bosom to bosom.

Nay, indeed, wisdom, knowledge, and skill pass from man even into the ox and the ass. The untrained horse, rough and unformed, becomes of good easy paces and docile; the bear dances, and the goat also salutes. From men the desire of doing something enters into the dog: he becomes a shepherd, or a hunter, or a guard.

Every moment a new species appears in the bosom: sometimes a demon, sometimes an angel, and sometimes wild beasts.

From that wonderful forest with which every lion is acquainted there is a hidden road to that snare, the bosoms of men.

MASNAVI

11

The Nature of Wisdom

May God grant to me to speak properly,
And to have thoughts worthy of what he has given;
For it is he that guides wisdom
And directs the wise.
For in his hand are we and our words,
All understanding and knowledge of trades.
For it is he that has given me unerring knowledge of what is,
To know the constitution of the world and the working of the
    elements;
The beginning and end and middle of periods of time,
The alternations of the solstices and the changes of the seasons,
The cycles of the years and the positions of the stars,
The natures of animals and the dispositions of wild beasts,
The powers of spirits and the designs of men,
The varieties of plants and the virtues of roots;
All that was secret or manifest I learned,
For wisdom, the fashioner of all things, taught me.
For there is in her a spirit that is intelligent, holy,
Unique, manifold, subtle,
Mobile, clear, undefiled,
Distinct, beyond harm, loving the good, keen,
Unhindered, beneficent, philanthropic,
Firm, sure, free from care,
All-powerful, all-seeing,
And interpenetrating all spirits
That are intelligent, pure, and most subtle.
For wisdom is more mobile than any motion,
And she penetrates and permeates everything, because she is so
    pure;
For she is the breath of the power of God,
And a pure emanation of his almighty glory;
Therefore nothing defiled can enter into her.

THE WISDOM OF SOLOMON 7:15-25

A Saint's Prayer

I knew a certain holy man who prayed thus. He used to say nothing before these words, but simply thus:

We give Thee thanks for all Thy benefits shown forth upon us, the unworthy, from the first day until the present; for what we know and what we know not; for the seen, for the unseen; for those in deed, those in word; those with our wills, those against our wills; for all that has been bestowed upon the unworthy, even us; for tribulations, for refreshments, for hell, for punishments, for the kingdom of heaven. We beseech Thee to keep our soul holy, having a pure conscience: an end worthy of Thy loving-kindness. Thou that loved us so as to give the Only-Begotten for us, grant us to become worthy of Thy love; give us wisdom in Thy word and in Thy fear, O Only-Begotten Christ! Inspire the strength that is from Thee, Thou that gavest Thy Only-Begotten for us, and has sent Thy Holy Spirit for the remission of our sins. If in ought we have willfully or unwillingly transgressed, pardon, and impute it not. Remember all that call upon Thy name in truth; remember all that wish us well or the contrary, for we are all men.

Then having added the prayer of the Faithful, he there ended; having made that prayer as a kind of summing up, and a binding together for all. For God bestows many benefits upon us, even against our wills; many also, and these greater, without our knowledge even. For when we pray for one thing and He does the reverse it is plain that He does us good, even when we know it not.

ST. JOHN CHRYSOSTOM

DAY 16   HINDUISM

Who Is a Kinsman

Even an enemy, if he performs a kindness,
Should be esteemed a kinsman.
Even a kinsman, if he does harm,

Should be considered a foe.
An illness, though bred in the body,
Works mischief, while a medicine
From some far forest does a friendly work.

Just as the traveler, finding the shade
Of a sheltering tree, rests and goes his way,
So men meet friends, then part with them forever.

You are a stream whose sacred ford is
Self-restraint; its water is truthfulness,
Its banks are virtue, its waves are love.
Wash yourself in this stream,
For mere water can never purify the inner man.

HITOPADESA

DAY 17   BUDDHISM
The Easy Life and the Hard

Life is easy to live for a man without shame, a crow hero, a
mischief-maker, an insulting, bold, and wretched fellow.

But life is hard to live for a modest man, who always looks for
what is pure, who is disinterested, quiet, spotless, and intelligent.

He who destroys life, who speaks untruth, who in this world
takes what is not given him, who goes to another man's wife—
and the man who gives himself to drinking intoxicating liquors—
he, even in this world, digs up his own root.

DHAMMAPADA

DAY 18   CONFUCIANISM
The Meaning of Sacrifice

Of all the methods for the good ordering of men, there is none
more urgent than the use of ceremonies. Ceremonies are of five
kinds, and there is none of them more important than sacrifice.

Sacrifice is not a thing coming to a man from without; it issues
from within him, and has its birth in his heart. When the heart

14

is deeply moved, expression is given to it by ceremonies; and hence, only men of ability and virtue can completely show forth the idea of sacrifice.

The sacrifices of such men have their own blessing, not indeed what the world calls blessing. Blessing here means perfection; it is the name given to the complete and natural discharge of all duties. When nothing is left incomplete or improperly discharged, this is what we call perfection, implying the doing of everything that should be done in one's internal self; and externally, the performance of everything according to the proper method. There is a fundamental agreement between a loyal subject in his service of his ruler and a filial son in his service of his parents. In the supernal sphere, there is a compliance with what is due to the repose and expansion of the energies of nature; in the external sphere, a compliance with what is due to rulers and elders; in the internal sphere, the filial service of parents. All this constitutes what is called perfection.

It is only the able and virtuous man who can attain to this perfection and can sacrifice when he has attained to it. Hence in his sacrifices, such a man brings into exercise all sincerity and good faith, with all right-heartedness and reverence; he offers the proper things, . . . does everything suitably to the season. Thus intelligently does he offer his sacrifices, without seeking for anything to be gained by them.

LI KI

DAY 19   BUDDHISM
The Faults of Others

The fault of others is easily perceived, but that of oneself is difficult to perceive; a man winnows his neighbor's faults like chaff, but his own fault he hides, as a cheat hides the bad die from the gambler.

If a man looks after the faults of others, and is always inclined to be offended, his own passions will grow, and he is far from the destruction of passions.

DHAMMAPADA

15

Charity

In the Name of God, the Merciful, the Compassionate
Hast thou seen him who cries lies to the Doom?
That is he who repulses the orphan
and urges not the feeding of the needy.

So woe to those that pray
and are heedless of their prayers,
to those who make display
and refuse charity.

THE KORAN

The Delinquent Son

A father complained to the Besht that his son had forsaken God. "What, Rabbi, shall I do?"

"Love him more than ever," was the Besht's reply.

HASIDIC STORY

Why Mourn?

When Chuang Tzu's wife died, Hui Tzu went to condole. He found the widower sitting on the ground, singing, with his legs spread out at a right angle, and beating time on a bowl.

"To live with your wife," exclaimed Hui Tzu, "and see your eldest son grow up to be a man, and then not to shed a tear over her corpse,—this would be bad enough. But to drum on a bowl, and sing; surely this is going too far."

"Not at all," replied Chuang Tzu. "When she died, I could not help being affected by her death. Soon, however, I remembered that she had already existed in a previous state before birth,

16

without form, or even substance; that while in that unconditioned condition, substance was added to spirit; that this substance then assumed form; and that the next stage was birth. And now, by virtue of a further change, she is dead, passing from one phase to another like the sequence of spring, summer, autumn, and winter. And while she is thus lying asleep in eternity, for me to go about weeping and wailing would be to proclaim myself ignorant of these natural laws. Therefore I refrain."

CHUANG TZU

DAY 23   EGYPTIAN RELIGION

The Riches of God

Do not neglect a stranger with thy oil jar
That it be doubled before thy brethren.
God desires respect for the poor
More than the honoring of the exalted.

For man is the clay and straw,
And the god is his builder.
He is tearing down and building up every day.
He makes a thousand men poor as he wishes
Or he makes a thousand men as overseers.
When he is in his hour of life,
How joyful is he who reaches the west
When he is safe in the hand of the god.
Better is poverty in the hand of the god
Than riches in a storehouse.
Better is bread when the heart is happy
Than riches with sorrow.

THE INSTRUCTIONS OF AMEN-EM-OPET

DAY 24   CHRISTIANITY

Paradise Is God's Will

What is Paradise? All things that are; for all are goodly and pleasant, and therefore may fitly be called a Paradise. It is said

17

also, that Paradise is an outer court of Heaven. Even so this world is truly an outer court of the Eternal, or of Eternity, and specially whatever in Time or any temporal things or creatures manifests or reminds us of God or Eternity; for the creatures are a guide and a path to God and Eternity. Thus this world is an outer court of Eternity, and therefore it may well be called a Paradise, for it is such in truth. And in this Paradise, all things are lawful, save one tree and the fruits thereof. That is to say: of all things that are, nothing is forbidden and nothing is contrary to God but one thing only: that is, Self-will, or to will otherwise than as the Eternal Will would have it. Remember this. For God says to Adam, that is, to every man, "Whatever you are, or do, or leave undone, or whatever happens, is all lawful and not forbidden if it is not done from or according to your will, but for the sake of and according to My will. But all that is done from your own will is contrary to the Eternal Will."

THEOLOGIA GERMANICA

The Self

If a man hold himself dear, let him watch himself carefully; during one at least out of the three watches, a wise man should be watchful.

Let each man direct himself first to what is proper, then let him teach others; thus a wise man will not suffer.

If a man make himself as he teaches others to be, then, being himself well subdued, he may subdue others; for one's own self is difficult to subdue.

Self is the lord of self; who else could be the lord? With self well subdued, a man finds a lord such as few can find.

The evil done by one's self, self-begotten, self-bred, crushes the foolish, as a diamond breaks even a precious stone.

He whose wickedness is very great brings himself down to that state where his enemy wishes him to be, as a creeper does with the tree which it surrounds.

Bad deeds, and deeds hurtful to ourselves, are easy to do; what is beneficial and good, that is very difficult to do.

The foolish man who scorns the rule of the venerable (Arhat), of the elect (Ariya), of the virtuous, and follows a false doctrine —he bears fruit to his own destruction, like the fruits of the Katthaka reed.

By one's self the evil is done; by one's self one suffers; by one's self evil is left undone; by one's self one is purified. The pure and impure stand and fall by themselves; no one can purify another.

Let no one forget his own duty for the sake of another's, however great; let a man, after he has discerned his own duty, be always attentive to his duty.

DHAMMAPADA

DAY 26   JUDAISM
The End Is Like the Beginning

A fox saw a fine vineyard and lusted after its grapes. But the palings were placed close together, and the fox was too bulky to creep between them. For three days he fasted, and when he had grown thin, he entered into the vineyard. He feasted upon the grapes, forgetting everything but his enjoyment; and lo, he had grown stout and was unable to leave the scene of his feast. So for three days more he fasted, and when he had again grown thin, he passed through the palings and stood outside the vineyard, as thin as when he entered.

So with man; poor and naked he enters the world, poor and naked does he leave.

RABBINICAL ANA

DAY 27   CONFUCIANISM
The Nature of Man

I like fish and I also like bear's paws. If I cannot have the two together, I will let the fish go and take the bear's paws. Similarly, I like life and I also like righteousness. If I cannot keep the two together, I will let life go and choose righteousness.

19

I like life indeed, but there is that which I like more than life, and therefore I will not seek to possess it by any improper means. I dislike death indeed, but there is that which I dislike more than death, and therefore there are occasions when I will not avoid danger.

If among the things which man likes, there was nothing he liked more than life, why should he not use every means by which he could preserve it? If among the things which man dislikes, there was nothing which he disliked more than death, why should he not do everything by which he could avoid danger? . . .

Therefore, men have that which they like more than life, and that which they dislike more than death. They are not men of distinguished talents and virtue only who have this mental nature. All men have it; what belongs to such men is simply that they do not lose it. . . .

MENCIUS

DAY 28

JUDAISM-
CHRISTIANITY

What Is Man?

O Lord, our Lord, how majestic is thy name in all the earth! Thou whose glory above the heavens is chanted by the mouth of babes and infants, thou hast founded a bulwark because of thy foes, to still the enemy and the avenger. When I look at thy heavens, the work of thy fingers, the moon and the stars which thou hast established; what is man that thou art mindful of him and the son of man that thou dost care for him? Yet thou hast made him little less than God, and dost crown him with glory and honor. Thou hast given him dominion over the works of thy hands; thou hast put all things under his feet, all sheep and oxen, and also the beasts of the field, the birds of the air, and the fish of the sea, whatever passes along the paths of the sea. O Lord, our Lord, how majestic is thy name in all the earth!

PSALM 8

20

How Evil Appears Good

The gods defend not with a club or shield
The man they wish to favor—but endow him
With wisdom; and the man whom they intend
To ruin they deprive of understanding,
So that to him all things appear distorted.
Then, when his mind is dulled and he is ripe
To meet his doom, evil appears to him
Like good, and even fortunate events
Turn to his harm and tend to his destruction.

MAHABHARATA

Higher Than Mere Skill

Prince Huei's cook was cutting up a bullock. Every blow of his hand, every heave of his shoulders, every tread of his foot, every thrust of his knee, every *whshh* of rent flesh, every *chhk* of the chopper, was in perfect rhythm—rhythmical like the dance of the Mulberry Grove, simultaneous like the chords of Ching Shou.

"Well done!" cried the Prince. "Yours is skill indeed!"

"Sire," replied the cook, "I have always devoted myself to Tao. It is better than skill. When I first began to cut up bullocks, I saw before me *whole* bullocks. After three years' practice, I saw whole animals no more. And now I work with my mind and not with my eye. When my senses bid me stop, but my mind urges me on, I fall back upon eternal principles. I follow such openings or cavities as there may be, according to the natural constitution of the animal. I do not attempt to cut through the joints, still less through large bones.

"A good cook changes his chopper once a year, because he cuts. An ordinary cook, once a month, because he hacks. But I have had this chopper nineteen years, and although I have cut many thousands of bullocks, its edge is as if fresh from the whetstone.

For at the joints there are always interstices, and the edge of a chopper being without thickness, it remains only to insert that which is without thickness into such an interstice. By these means the interstice will be enlarged, and the blade will find plenty of room. It is thus that I have kept my chopper for nineteen years as though fresh from the whetstone.

"Nevertheless, when I come upon a hard part which is difficult to tackle, I am all caution. I fix my eye on it. I stay my hand, and gently apply my blade, until with a *hwah* the part yields like earth crumbling to the ground. Then I take out my chopper and stand up, and look around, and pause until with an air of triumph I wipe my chopper and put it carefully away."

"Bravo!" cried the Prince, "From the words of this cook I have learnt how to take care of my life."

CHUANG TZU

Nonattachment

My friend, wisdom lies
In abandoning heedlessness,
In turning the heart away from the worldly objects,
And in gathering provision for the hereafter
Before departure from this earth.

Wealthy men are narrow-hearted,
Others, discontented for all time,
Lament their misfortunes
Real and imagined.

The emancipated are freed
From bonds of being, and non-being:
They have broken the cage
And found their freedom,

They have emptied
The cup of desire;
They strive no more
For worldly greatness.

Freed from joy and sorrow
They have found their true self;
They dwell for ever more
In the wondrous realm of God.

THE INVOCATION OF SHEIKH ABDULLAH ANSARI

DAY 32   CHRISTIANITY
How to Bear with Others

In order to be satisfied even with the best people, we need to
be content with little, and to bear a great deal. Even the most
perfect people have many imperfections, and we ourselves have no
fewer. Our faults combined with theirs make mutual toleration
a difficult matter, but we can only "fulfill the law of Christ" by
"bearing one another's burdens." There must be a mutual, loving
forbearance. Frequent silence, habitual recollection, prayer, self-
detachment, giving up all critical tendencies, watchfulness to put
aside all the idle imaginations of jealous, fastidious self-love—all
these will go far to maintain peace and unity. How many troubles
we might save ourselves thereby! Happy he who neither gives
ear to himself nor to the idle talk of others!

Be content to lead a quiet life where God has placed you. Be
obedient, bear your little daily crosses—you need them, and it
is out of pure mercy that God lays them on you. The great thing
is thoroughly to despise yourself, and to be willing that others
should despise you, if God so will. Feed wholly on him. St.
Augustine says that his mother lived only on prayer. Do you the
same, and die to all else. But we can only live to God by continually dying to self.

FRANÇOIS DE FÉNELON

DAY 33   TAOISM
The Timeliness of Charity

Once Chuang Tzu was reduced to such extremities that he was
faced with starvation and was obliged to go to the Prince of Wei

23

and ask for some millet. "I am hoping before long," said the Prince of Wei, "to receive the rent money from the tenants in my fief. Then I shall be pleased to lend you three hundred pieces; will that be all right?" "On my way here yesterday," said Chuang Tzu, looking very indignant, "I suddenly heard a voice somewhere in the roadway calling for help. I looked round, and there in the cart track was a gudgeon. 'Gudgeon,' I said, 'what are you doing there?' 'I am an exile from the eastern seas,' said the gudgeon. 'Let me have a peck measure of water, and you will save my life.' 'I am hoping before long,' I said to it, 'to go south to Wu and Yüeh. I will ask the king to dam the western river, so that it may flow your way. Will that be all right?' 'I have lost my proper surroundings and have no place to call my own,' said the gudgeon. 'All the same, if you gave me a peck measure of water I could manage to keep alive. If instead of that you do what you propose, you might as well string me up at once in the dried-fish shop.'"

CHUANG TZU

DAY 34   JUDAISM
The Cripple and the Porter

A famous musician once came to a town and posted announcements for a concert. All the well-to-do folk hurried to buy their seats. In the town there lived a man who was a great lover of music, but both his legs were crippled and he was so poor that he had not the price of a seat. He had just about enough for standing room, which was of no use to him. However, he could not bear to miss this event, and for a few groschen he induced a poor porter to carry him, perched on his back, to the concert hall. And thus seated on the porter's shoulders he listened with unbounded delight. But now and then he was so carried away by the player's genius and the beauty of the music that he forgot where he was sitting. He danced about, clapping his hands, until the porter began to complain. "You are breaking my neck. Stop

24

kicking my sides. Don't press so on my shoulders!" But the cripple forgot these complaints in the intervals of playing until finally the porter said, "I cannot bear you any longer. I am going to set you down." The cripple implored his indulgence and in the next intermission asked the porter to carry him to a nearby wine-shop. There he ordered a large brandy for the porter and they returned to the concert hall. Now the porter, cheered and en-livened by the drink, was himself so touched by the music that he swayed and capered to its rhythms, no longer mindful of the antics of his burden. And thus a blissful peace was established be-tween them, and both enjoyed the concert to its end.

Thus it is clear that the important thing on the Sabbath is in-deed to praise God with a pure soul. But the soul is unfortunately crippled without the body; lacking the body it can neither praise nor thank God. Now, should the body be impatient, dissatisfied, the soul will not achieve its Sabbath delight. Hence we are taught to satisfy the body, to cheer it with wine and good food, so that it too may be free to join the spirit in praise of the Almighty, to sustain the soul in joyful contemplation. Then only will the Sabbath be perfect.

RABBI SHOLEM

DAY 35   ISLAM
Breaking Promises

Take care not to promise something and then fail to perform it. The good you do to people should rather be in deed without any word. If you are forced to make a promise, take care not to break it, except from inability to fulfill it or from compulsion. To do so is one of the signs of hypocrisy and wickedness. Mu-hammad (God bless and preserve him) said: "There are three things, which, if a man practices secretly, he is a hypocrite, even though he fasts and performs the Worship: if, when he relates something, he lies; if, when he makes a promise, he breaks it; if, when he is given a trust, he betrays it."

AL GHAZALI

25

The Song of Creation

Then was not non-existent nor existent: there was no realm of
air, no sky beyond it.
What covered in, and where? and what gave shelter?
Was water there, unfathomed depth of water?

Death was not then, nor was there aught immortal: no sign was
there, the day's and night's divider.
That one thing, breathless, breathed by its own nature: apart from
it was nothing whatsoever.

Darkness there was: at first concealed in darkness, this All was
indiscriminated chaos.
All that existed then was void and formless: by the great power
of warmth was born that unit.

Thereafter rose desire in the beginning: Desire, the primal seed
and germ of spirit.
Sages who searched with their heart's thought, discovered the
existent's kinship in the non-existent.

Transversely was their severing line extended: what was above it
then, and what below it?
There were begetters, there were mighty forces, free action here
and energy up yonder.

Who verily knows and who can here declare it, whence it was
born and whence comes this creation?
The gods are later than this world's production. Who knows, then,
whence it first came into being?

He, the first origin of this creation, whether he formed it all or
did not form it,
Whose eye controls this world in highest heaven, he verily knows
it, or perhaps he knows it not.

RIGVEDA

The Accumulation of Good and Evil

If a man commits a sin, let him not do it again; let him not delight in sin: the accumulation of evil is painful. If a man does what is good, let him do it again; let him delight in it: the accumulation of good is delightful. Even an evildoer sees happiness as long as his evil deed does not ripen; but when his evil deed ripens, then he sees the evil. Even a good man sees evil days, so long as his good deed does not ripen; but when his good deed ripens, then does the good man see good things. Let no man think lightly of evil, saying in his heart, "It will not come nigh unto me." Even by the falling of drops of water a pot is filled; the fool becomes full of evil, even if he gathers it little by little. . . . He who has no wound on his hand may touch poison with his hand; poison does not affect one who has no wound; nor is there evil for one who does not commit evil. . . .

DHAMMAPADA

The Allegory of Old Age

Remember now thy Creator in the days of thy youth, while the evil days come not, nor the years draw nigh, when thou shalt say, I have no pleasure in them; while the sun, or the light, or the moon, or the stars, be not darkened, nor the clouds return after the rain: in the day when the keepers of the house shall tremble, and the strong men shall bow themselves, and the grinders cease because they are few, and those that look out of the windows be darkened. And the doors shall be shut in the streets, when the sound of the grinding is low, and he shall rise up at the voice of the bird, and all the daughters of musick shall be brought low; also when they shall be afraid of that which is high, and fears shall be in the way, and the almond tree shall flourish, and the grasshopper shall be a burden, and desire shall fail: because man goeth to his long home, and the mourners go about the streets: or ever the silver cord be loosed, or the golden bowl be broken, or the pitcher be broken at the fountain, or the wheel broken at the cistern. Then shall the dust return to the earth as it was: and the spirit shall return unto God who gave it. Vanity of vanities, saith the preacher; all is vanity.

ECCLESIASTES 12:1-8

DAY 39 CHRISTIANITY

The Significance of Prayer

I take it for granted that every Christian that is in health is up early in the morning, for it is much more reasonable to suppose a person up early because he is a Christian than because he is a labourer, or a tradesman, or a servant, or has business that wants him.

We naturally conceive some abhorrence of a man that is in bed when he should be at his labour or in his shop. We cannot tell how to think anything good of him who is such a slave to drowsiness as to neglect his business for it.

Let this therefore teach us to conceive how odious we must appear in the sight of Heaven if we are in bed, shut up in sleep and darkness, when we should be praising God, and all such slaves to drowsiness as to neglect our devotions for it.

For if he is to be blamed as a slothful drone that rather chooses the lazy indulgence of sleep than to perform his proper share of worldly business, how much more is he to be reproached that would rather be folded up in a bed than be raising up his heart to God in acts of praise and adoration!

Prayer is the nearest approach to God, and the highest enjoyment of Him, that we are capable of in this life.

It is the noblest exercise of the soul, the most exalted of our best facilities and the highest imitation of the blessed inhabitants of Heaven.

When our hearts are full of God, sending up holy desires to

the throne of grace, we are then in the highest state, we are upon the utmost heights of human greatness; we are not before kings and princes, but in the presence and audience of the Lord of all the world, and can be no higher till death is swallowed up in glory.

WILLIAM LAW

DAY 40   ISLAM

Lying

Keep your tongue from lying, whether in earnest or in jest. Do not accustom yourself to lying in jest, for it may lead you to lying in earnest. Lying is one of the sources of the greater sins, and, if you come to be known as a liar, your uprightness becomes worthless, your word is not accepted, and [men's] eyes scorn and despise you. If you want to know the foulness of lying for yourself, consider the lying of someone else and how you shun it and despise the man who lies and regard his communication as foul. Do the same with regard to all your own vices, for you do not realize the foulness of your own vices from your own case, but from someone else's. What you hold bad in another man, others will undoubtedly hold bad in you. Do not therefore be complacent about that in yourself.

AL GHAZALI

DAY 41   TAOISM

The Three Treasures

All the world says to me: "Great as Tao is, it resembles no description (form)." Because it is great, therefore it resembles no description. If it resembled any description it would have long since become small.

I have three treasures, which I hold and keep safe:
The first is called love;

29

The second is called moderation;
The third is called not venturing to go ahead of the world.
Being loving, one can be brave;
Being moderate, one can be ample;
Not venturing to go ahead of the world, one can be the chief
of all officials.
Instead of love, one has only bravery;
Instead of moderation, one has only amplitude:
Instead of keeping behind, one goes ahead:
These lead to nothing but death.
For he who fights with love will win the battle;
He who defends with love will be secure.
Heaven will save him, and protect him with love.

TAO-TE-KING

Two Kinds of Love

At times a man rests on his bed, and it appears to his family as though he were asleep, but he spends this hour in solitude with his Creator, blessed be He. That is a high rung, that he beholds the Creator at all times with the eye of his insight, as he sees another man. And consider this: if you persevere in a pure thought, then the Creator also looks at you, as a man looks at you.

There are two kinds of love. One man loves the acts and speeches of his clever son and boasts to his friends that he does and says clever things; the other loves his son himself whatever he may say and do. So it is with the love of God for man. When a proven man fulfills commands and good works in great wisdom, then God loves his deed and is present to all his doings, and thus the externals of the world are bound to God. But when the proven man himself adheres to God, then God loves him himself even though he does not accomplish his works in wisdom, rather walks in great simplicity and cleaves to God; for just this reason God loves him. And thus the inwardness of this world is raised to God.

MARTIN BUBER

Consciousness

Once upon a time a conch-blower, taking his conch, came to a border district and, standing in a village, blew on his conch three times, laid it aside and sat down. The people wondered who had made that lovely and charming sound, and they asked the conch-blower. He told them it was the conch and that was its lovely and charming sound. They laid the conch on its back and said: "Speak, conch, speak." But it gave never a sound. So they laid it curving downwards, then on one side, then on the other, and they stood it upright and topsy-turvy and they struck it on all its sides with their hands, with clods of earth, sticks and knives, saying: "Speak, conch, speak." But it gave never a sound. The conch-blower thought these border people were too stupid to see the conch's sound in such senseless ways. And while they watched he picked it up, blew on it three times and went away with it. Then these border people thought: "So long as this conch is accompanied by a man and by exertion and by wind it makes a sound. But so long as it is accompanied neither by a man nor by exertion nor by wind it makes no sound."

Even so, so long as this body is accompanied by life and heat and consciousness, so long does it walk backwards and forwards, stand still and sit and lie down, see, hear, smell, taste, touch and discern mental states with the mind. But so long as this body is accompanied neither by life nor heat nor consciousness, it does none of these things.

DIGHA-NIKAYA

DAY 44   JUDAISM-
                                              CHRISTIANITY
Despisers of the World

Woe to those who call evil good and good evil,
Who put darkness for light and light for darkness,
Who put bitter for sweet and sweet for bitter!

Woe to those who are wise in their own eyes,
And shrewd in their own sight!
Woe to those who are heroes at drinking wine,
And valiant men in mixing strong drink,
Who acquit the guilty for a bribe,
And deprive the innocent of his right!

Therefore, as the tongue of fire devours the stubble,
And as dry grass sinks down in the flame,
So their root will be as rottenness,
And their blossom go up like dust;
For they have rejected the law of the Lord of hosts,
And have despised the word of the Holy One of Israel.

ISAIAH 5:20-24

DAY 45   HINDUISM
No Distinctions in the Divine Sight

As a wet nurse in a rich family brings up the child of her master, loving the baby as if it were her own, but knows well that she has no claim upon it; so think also that you are but trustees and guardians of your children whose real father is the Lord God in heaven.

When the knowledge of Self is gained, all fetters fall off of themselves. Then there is no distinction between a Brahman and a Sudra, a high caste or a low caste. In that state the sacred-thread-sign of caste falls away of itself. But so long as a man has the consciousness of distinction and difference, he should not forcibly throw it off.

The spiritual-minded belong to a caste of their own, irrespective of all social conventions.

When a man is on the plains he sees the lowly grass and the mighty pine trees and says, "How big is the tree and how small is the grass!" But when he ascends the mountain and looks from its high peak on the plain below, the mighty pine tree and the lowly grass blend into one indistinguishable mass of green verdure. So in the sight of the worldly there are differences of rank and position—one is a king, another is a cobbler; one a father, another a son, and so on—but when the divine sight is opened, all appear as equal and one, and there remains no distinction of good and bad, high and low.

RAMAKRISHNA

DAY 46   CONFUCIANISM
The Man with the Heart of a Child

Acts of propriety which are not really proper, and acts of righteousness which are not really righteous, the great man does not do.

Those who keep the Mean, train up those who do not, and those who have abilities, train up those who have not, and hence men rejoice in having fathers and elder brothers who are possessed of virtue and talent. If they who keep the Mean spurn those who do not, and they who have abilities spurn those who have not, then the space between them—those so gifted and the ungifted—will not admit an inch.

Men must be decided on what they will *not* do, and then they are able to act with vigor in what they ought to do. . . .

The great man does not think beforehand of his words that they may be sincere, nor of his actions that they may be resolute; he simply speaks and does what is right.

The great man is he who does not lose his child's heart. . . .

That whereby man differs from the lower animals is but small. The mass of people cast it away, while superior men preserve it.

MENCIUS

DAY 47   CHRISTIANITY
The Beatitudes

And seeing the multitudes, he went up into a mountain: and when he was set, his disciples came unto him: and he opened his mouth, and taught them, saying, blessed are the poor in spirit: for their's is the kingdom of heaven. Blessed are they that mourn:

for they shall be comforted. Blessed are the meek: for they shall inherit the earth. Blessed are they which do hunger and thirst after righteousness: for they shall be filled. Blessed are the merciful: for they shall obtain mercy. Blessed are the pure in heart: for they shall see God. Blessed are the peacemakers: for they shall be called the children of God. Blessed are they which are persecuted for righteousness' sake: for their's is the kingdom of heaven. Blessed are ye, when men shall revile you, and persecute you, and shall say all manner of evil against you falsely, for my sake. Rejoice and be exceeding glad: for great is your reward in heaven: for so persecuted they the prophets which were before you.

Ye are the salt of the earth: but if the salt have lost his savour, wherewith shall it be salted? it is thenceforth good for nothing, but to be cast out, and to be trodden under foot of men. Ye are the light of the world. A city that is set on an hill cannot be hid. Neither do men light a candle, and put it under a bushel, but on a candlestick; and it giveth light unto all that are in the house. Let your light so shine before men, that they may see your good works, and glorify your Father which is in heaven.

MATTHEW 5:1-16

DAY 48   JUDAISM
The Joyous Mother's Altars

Once a Jewish mother with her seven sons suffered martyrdom at the hands of the Emperor. Each of the sons, when ordered by the latter to do homage to the idols of the Emperor, declined, and each justified his disobedience by quoting a simple text from the sacred Scriptures. When the seventh was brought forth, it is related that Caesar, for appearance' sake, offered to spare him if only he would stoop and pick up a ring from the ground which had been dropped on purpose. "Alas for you, O Caesar!" answered the boy; "if you are so zealous for your honor, how much more zealous ought we to be for the honor of the Holy One—blessed be He!" On his being led away to the place of execution, the mother craved and obtained leave to give him a farewell kiss. "Go, my child," said she, "and say to Abraham, 'You built an altar for the sacrifice of one son, but I have erected altars for seven sons.'" She then turned away and threw herself down headlong from the roof and expired, when the echo of a voice was heard exclaiming (Psalm 113:9), "The mother of the children rejoices."

GITTIN

DAY 49   TAOISM
The Pigs' Point of View

The Grand Augur, in his ceremonial robes, approached the slaughterhouse and thus addressed the pigs:

"How can you object to dying? I shall fatten you for three months. I shall discipline myself for ten days and fast for three. I shall strew fine grass, and place you bodily upon a carved sacrificial dish. Does this not satisfy you?"

Then, speaking from the pigs' point of view, he continued, "It is better perhaps after all to live on bran and escape slaughter."

"But then," added he, speaking from his own point of view, "to enjoy honor when alive one would readily die on a warshield or in the headsman's basket."

So he rejected the pigs' point of view and adopted his own point of view. In what sense then was he different from the pigs?

CHUANG TZU

DAY 50   ISLAM
A Prayer for Good Behavior

Let us beseech God to help us to self-control: he who lacks self-
control is deprived of the grace of the Lord.
The undisciplined man does not corrupt himself alone: he sets
the whole world afire.
Whatever befalls thee of gloom and sorrow is the result of thy
irreverence and insolence.
Anyone behaving with irreverence in the path of the Friend is a
brigand who robs men: he is no man.

Through discipline Heaven was filled with light, through discipline the Angels became immaculate and holy.
By reason of irreverence the sun is eclipsed, and insolence caused 'Azrazil to be turned back from the door.

JALALU'L-DIN RUMI

The Goodness of Man's Nature

The philosopher Kaou said, "Man's nature is like the *ke* willow, and righteousness is like a cup or bowl. Fashioning benevolence and righteousness out of man's nature is like making cups and bowls from the *ke* willow."

Mencius replied, "Can you make cups and bowls and still leave the nature of the willow untouched? You must do violence and injury to the willow before you can make cups and bowls with it. If so, on your principles, you must in the same way do violence and injury to humanity in order to fashion from it benevolence and righteousness! Your words, alas, would certainly lead all men on to reckon benevolence and righteousness to be calamities."

The philosopher Kaou said, "Man's nature is like water whirling around in a corner. Open a passage for it to the east, and it will flow to the east; open a passage for it to the west, and it will flow to the west. Man's nature is indifferent to good and evil, just as the water is indifferent to the east and west."

Mencius replied, "Water indeed will flow indifferently to the east or west, but will it flow indifferently up or down? The tendency of man's nature to good is like the tendency of water to flow downwards. There are none who do not have this tendency to good, just as all water flows downwards.

"Now by striking water and causing it to leap up, you may make it go over your forehead, and, by damaging and leading it, you may force it up a hill; but are such movements according to the nature of water? It is the force applied which causes them. When men are made to do what is not good, their nature is dealt with in this way."

MENCIUS

Alcoholism

Who has woe? Who has sorrow? Who has strife? Who has com-
    plaining?
Who has wounds without cause? Who has redness of eyes?
Those who tarry long over wine, those who go to try mixed wine.
Do not look at wine when it is red, when it sparkles in the cup
    and goes down smoothly.
At last it bites like a serpent, and stings like an adder.
Your eyes will see strange things, and your mind utter perverse
    things.
You will be like one who lies down in the midst of the sea, like
    one who lies on the top of a mast.
"They struck me," you will say, "but I was not hurt; they beat
    me, but I did not feel it.
When shall I awake? I will seek another drink."

PROVERBS 23:29-35

The Man Worthy of Respect

A man is not just if he carries a matter by violence; no, he
who distinguishes both right and wrong, who is learned and leads
others, not by violence but by law and equity, and who is
guarded by the law and intelligent, he is called just.

A man is not learned because he talks much; he who is patient,
free from hatred and fear, he is called learned.

A man is not an elder because his head is grey; his age may be
ripe, but he is called "old-in-vain."

He in whom there is truth, virtue, love, restraint, moderation,
he who is free from impurity and is wise, he is called an elder.

An envious, greedy, dishonest man does not become respectable
by means of much talking only, or by the beauty of his complex-
ion.

37

He in whom all this is destroyed, and taken out with the very
root, he, when freed from hatred, and wise, is called respectable.

DHAMMAPADA

True Righteousness Is Empathy

This is the sum of true righteousness—
Treat others as you would like to be treated.
Do nothing to your neighbor that hereafter
You would not have your neighbor do to you.
In causing pleasure, or in giving pain,
In doing good or injury to others,
In granting or refusing a request,
A man obtains a proper rule of action
By looking on his neighbor as himself.

Before infirmities creep over your flesh;
Before decay impairs your strength and mars
The beauty of your limbs; before the Ender,
Whose charioteer is sickness, hastes toward you,
Breaks up your fragile frame and ends your life,
Lay up the only treasure: do good deeds;
Practice sobriety and self-control;
Amass that wealth which thieves cannot rob you of,
Nor tyrants seize, which follows you at death,
Which never wastes away, nor is corrupted.

MAHABHARATA

Necessity and Freedom

Man is, and yet is not, involved in the flux of nature and time.
He is a creature subject to nature's necessities and limitations;
but he is also a free spirit who knows of the brevity of his years
and by this knowledge transcends the temporal by some capacity
within himself. Man "brings his years to an end as a tale that is

told," having an even shorter life span than some dumb creatures. But the sense of melancholy which the anticipation of death induces in the human spirit is not known in the animal world. To brood either anxiously or with studied and learned serenity upon the fact that man is as "the grass which flourisheth in the morning and in the evening is cut down and withereth" is to reveal the whole dimension of existence which distinguishes man from the animal world.

Man's ability to transcend the flux of nature gives him the capacity to make history. Human history is rooted in the natural process but it is something more than either the determined sequences of natural causation or the capricious variations and occurrences of the natural world. It is compounded of natural necessity and human freedom. Man's freedom to transcend the natural flux gives him the possibility of grasping a span of time in his consciousness and thereby of knowing history. It also enables him to change, reorder and transmute the causal sequences of nature and thereby to *make* history.

REINHOLD NIEBUHR

DAY 56 CHRISTIANITY
Our Attitude to the Dying

Our attitude to all men would be Christian if we regarded them as though they were dying and determined our relation to them in the light of death, both of their death and our own. A person who is dying calls forth a special kind of feeling. Our attitude to him is at once softened and lifted onto a higher plane. We can then feel compassion for people whom we do not love. But every man is dying, I too am dying and must never forget about death.

NIKOLAI BERDYAEV

DAY 57 ISLAM
The Secret of Names

A man gave a diram to four persons. One of them, a Persian, said, "I will spend this on 'angur.' "

Another of them was an Arab; he said, "No, you rogue; I want 'inab,' not 'angur.' "

A third was a Turk; he said, "I do not want 'inab,' dear friend, I want 'uzum.' "

The fourth was a Greek; he said, "Stop this altercation; I wish for 'istafil.' "

Those persons began to fight against one another, because they were ignorant of the secret of names. Through sheer ignorance they struck one another with their fists; they were full of ignorance and devoid of knowledge.

If one who knew the inner truth, an estimable man versed in many tongues, had been there, he would have reconciled them. He would have said, "With this one diram I will gratify the desire of all of you. If in all sincerity you entrust your hearts to me, this diram of yours will do so much for you. Your one diram will become as four, which is what is wanted; four enemies will become as one by concord. The words of each of you lead you to contention and disagreement; my words bring you agreement. Therefore be you silent, keep silence, in order that I may be your tongue in speech."

Although your words appear uniform and in harmony, they are the source in their effect of contention and anger.

MASNAVI

DAY 58   CONFUCIANISM
Watchfulness in Solitude

What is meant by "making the thoughts sincere" is allowing no self-deception, as when we hate a bad smell, and as when we love what is beautiful. This is called self-enjoyment. Therefore, the superior man must be watchful over himself when he is alone.

There is no evil to which the mean man, dwelling retired, will not proceed, but when he sees a superior man, he instantly tries to disguise himself, concealing his evil, and displaying what is good. The other beholds him as if he saw his heart and veins— of what use is his disguise? This is an instance of the saying,

40

"What truly is inside will be manifested outside." Therefore, the superior man must be watchful over himself when he is alone.

THE GREAT LEARNING

DAY 59   BUDDHISM
Teachings from the Law

Silently shall I endure abuse as the elephant in battle endures the arrow sent from the bow: for the world is ill-natured.

They lead a tamed elephant to battle, the king mounts a tamed elephant; the tamed is the best among men, he who silently endures abuse.

Mules are good, if tamed, and noble Sindhu horses, and elephants with large tusks; but he who tames himself is better still.

If a man becomes fat and a great eater, if he is sleepy and rolls himself about, that fool, like a hog fed on wash, is born again and again.

This mind of mine went formerly wandering about as it liked, as it listed, as it pleased; but I shall now hold it in thoroughly, as the rider who holds the hook holds in the furious elephant.

Be not thoughtless, watch your thoughts! Draw yourself out of the evil way, like an elephant sunk in mud.

If a man find a prudent companion who walks with him, is wise, and lives soberly, he may walk with him, overcoming all dangers, happy, but considerate.

If a man find no prudent companion who walks with him, is wise, and lives soberly, let him walk alone, like a king who has left his conquered country behind, like an elephant in the forest.

It is better to live alone, there is no companionship with a fool; let a man walk alone, let him commit no sin, having few wishes, like an elephant in the forest.

DHAMMAPADA

Partiality

Rabbi Ishmael, son of Rabbi Yossi, had a gardener who regularly brought him a basket of grapes every Friday. Bringing it once on a Thursday, the Rabbi asked him why he had come a day earlier. "My Lord," said the gardener, "having a lawsuit before you today, I thought I might save myself the journey tomorrow." At this the Rabbi both refused to take the basket of grapes, though they were really his own, and declined to act as judge in the trial. Instead, he appointed two rabbis to judge the case, and while they were examining the evidence in the litigation, he kept pacing up and down and saying to himself, if the gardener were sharp he might say so-and-so in his own behalf. He was at one time on the point of speaking in defense of his gardener, when he checked himself and said, "Those who take bribes may well look to their souls. If I feel partial, though I have not even taken a bribe of what was my own, how perverted must be the disposition of those who receive bribes at the hands of others!"

KETHUBOTH

All Life Is a Dream

Those who dream of a banquet wake to lamentation and sorrow. Those who dream of lamentation and sorrow wake to join the hunt. While they dream, they do not know that they dream. Some will even interpret the very dream they are dreaming, and only when they awake do they know it was a dream. By and by comes the Great Awakening, and then we find out that this life is really a great dream. Fools think they are awake now, and flatter themselves that they know if they are really princes or peasants. Confucius and you are both dreams; and I who say you are dreams, I am but a dream myself. This is a paradox. Tomorrow a sage may arise to explain it, but that tomorrow will not be until ten thousand generations have gone by. . . .

Once upon a time, I, Chuang Tzu, dreamt I was a butterfly, fluttering hither and thither, to all intents and purposes a butterfly. I was conscious only of following my fancies as a butterfly, and was unconscious of my individuality as a man. Suddenly I awoke, and there I lay, myself again. Now I do not know whether I was then a man dreaming I was a butterfly, or whether I am now a butterfly dreaming I am a man.

CHUANG TZU

DAY 62   JAINISM

The Paradox of Riches

Men who acquire wealth by evil deeds will lose it,
    falling into the snares of their passions,
        and being held captive by their hatred.

Wealth will not protect a careless man
    in this world or in the next.

If somebody should give the whole earth to one man,
    he would not have enough,
        so difficult is it to satisfy anybody.
            Your desires increase with your means.

If there were numberless mountains of gold and silver,
    they would not satisfy a greedy man,
        for his avidity is boundless like space.

What avail riches for the practice of religion?

If the whole world and all treasures were yours,
    you would still not be satisfied,
        nor would all this be able to save you.

UTTARA DHYAYANA SUTRA

43

Seeking the Lord's Will

"My son, thou hast still many things to learn, which thou hast not learned well yet."

"What are they, Lord?"

"To place thy desire altogether in subjection to My good pleasure, and not to be a lover of thyself, but an earnest seeker of My will. Thy desires often excite and urge thee forward; but consider with thyself whether thou art not more moved for thine own objects than for My honour. If it is Myself that thou seekest, thou shalt be well content with whatsoever I shall ordain; but if any pursuit of thine own lieth hidden within thee, behold it is this which hindereth and weigheth thee down.

"Beware, therefore, lest thou strive too earnestly after some desire which thou hast conceived, without taking counsel of Me; lest haply it repent thee afterwards, and that displease thee which before pleased, and for which thou didst long as for a good. For not every affection which seems good is to be forthwith followed; neither is every opposite affection to be immediately avoided. Sometimes it is expedient to use restraint even in good desires and wishes, lest through importunity thou fall into distraction of mind, lest through want of discipline thou become a stumbling block to others, or lest by the resistance of others thou be suddenly disturbed and brought to confusion.

"Sometimes indeed, it is needful to use violence, and manfully to strive against the sensual appetite, and not to consider what the flesh may or may not will; but rather to strive after this, that it may become subject, however unwillingly, to the spirit. And for so long it ought to be chastised and compelled to undergo slavery, even until it be ready for all things, and learn to be contented with little, to be delighted with things simple, and never to murmur at any inconvenience."

THOMAS A KEMPIS

44

The Functions of the Ruler

Heaven produces the seasons. Earth produces all the sources of wealth. Man is begotten by his father and instructed by his teacher. The ruler correctly uses these four agencies, and therefore he stands in the place where there is no error.

Hence the ruler is he to whose brightness men look; he does not seek to brighten men. . . . It is he whom men serve; he does not seek to serve men. If the ruler were to seek to brighten men he would fall into error. If he were to seek to nourish men, he would be unequal to the task. If he were to seek to serve men, he would be giving up his position. Therefore the people imitate the ruler, and we have their self-government; they nourish the ruler, and they find their security in doing so; they serve the ruler, and find their distinction in doing so. Thus it is by the universal application of the rules of propriety that the lot and duty of different classes are fixed; thus it is that men acting contrary to those rules would all have to account death a boon and life an evil.

Therefore the ruler, making use of the wisdom of others, will put away the cunning to which that wisdom might lead him; using their courage, he will put away passion; and using their benevolence, he will put away covetousness. . . .

Therefore when it is said that the ruler, being a sage, can look on everything under the sky as one family, and on everyone in the Middle States as one man, this does not mean that he will do so on premeditation and purpose. He must know men's feelings, lay open to them what they consider right, show clearly to them what is advantageous, and comprehend what are their calamities. Being so furnished, he is then able to effect the thing.

LI KI

Charity According to One's Means

It was said of Rabbi Tarphon that, though a wealthy man, he was not charitable according to his means. One time Rabbi Akiba said to him: "Shall I invest some money for real estate in a manner which will be very profitable?" Rabbi Tarphon answered in the affirmative, and brought to Rabbi Akiba four thousand denars in gold to be so applied. Rabbi Akiba immediately distributed the same among the poor. Sometime after this Rabbi Tarphon met Rabbi Akiba and asked him where the real estate which he had bought for him was situated. Akiba led him to the college, and showed him a little boy, who recited for them the 112th Psalm. When he reached the ninth verse—"He distributeth, he giveth to the needy, his righteousness endureth forever"—"There," said Akiba, "your property is with David, the king of Israel, who said, 'He distributeth, he giveth to the needy.'" "And why have you done this?" asked Tarphon. "Don't you know," answered Rabbi Akiba, "how Nakdimon, the son of Guryon, was punished because he did not give according to his means?" "Well," returned the other, "why didn't you tell me this; couldn't I have distributed my means without any aid?" "No," said Akiba, "it is a greater virtue to cause another to give than to give oneself." From this we may learn that he who is not charitable according to his means will be punished.

RABBINICAL ANA

"Three in the Morning"

A keeper of monkeys said with regard to their rations of chestnuts that each monkey was to have three in the morning and four at night. But at this the monkeys were very angry, so the keeper said they might have four in the morning and three at night, with which arrangement they were all well pleased. The actual number of the chestnuts remained the same, but there was an adaptation to the likes and dislikes of those concerned. Such is the principle of putting oneself into subjective relation with externals. Wherefore the true Sage, while regarding contraries as identical, adapts himself to the laws of Heaven.

CHUANG TZU

BUDDHISM

The Clouding of the Mind

Once upon a time, when Brahmadatta was king of Benares, the Bodhisattva was born in the family of a Brahmin magnifico. When he grew up, he studied under a far-famed teacher of Takkasila, where he learnt all magic charms. After returning to Benares he taught these charms to a large number of Brahmin and Kshatriya youths.

Among these youths was one young Brahmin who had learnt the three Vedas by heart; he became a master of ritual, and could repeat the whole of the sacred texts without stumbling in a single line. Eventually he married and settled down. Then household cares clouded his mind, and he was no longer able to repeat the sacred verses.

One day his teacher paid him a visit. "Well, young Sir," he inquired, "do you know all your verses by heart?" "Since I have been the head of a household," was the reply, "my mind has been clouded, and I cannot repeat them." "My son," said his teacher, "when the mind is clouded, no matter how perfectly the scriptures have been learnt, they will not stand out clear. But when the mind is serene there is no forgetting them." And thereupon he repeated the following verses:

Thick, muddy water will not show
Fish or shell or sand or gravel that may lie below;
    So with a clouded wit:
Nor your nor other's good is seen in it.

Clear, quiet waters ever show
All, be it fish or shell, that lies below;
So with unclouded wit:
Both your and other's good shows clear in it.

JATAKA

DAY 68 JUDAISM-
CHRISTIANITY

Greed Does Not Gratify

If you see in a province the poor oppressed and justice and right violently taken away, do not be amazed at the matter; for the high official is watched by a higher, and there are yet higher ones over them.

But in all, a king is an advantage to a land with cultivated fields. He who loves money will not be satisfied with money; nor he who loves wealth, with gain: this also is vanity. When goods increase, they increase who eat them; and what gain has their owner but to see them with his eyes? Sweet is the sleep of a laborer, whether he eats little or much; but the surfeit of the rich will not let him sleep. There is a grievous evil which I have seen under the sun: riches were kept by their owner to his hurt, and those riches were lost in a bad venture; and he is father of a son, but he has nothing in his hand. As he came from his mother's womb he shall go again, naked as he came, and shall take nothing for his toil, which he may carry away in his hand.

ECCLESIASTES 5:8-15

DAY 69 HINDUISM

The Influence of Bad Habits

A fisherwoman on her way home from a distant market was overtaken by a storm at nightfall, so she was compelled to take refuge in a florist's house near at hand. The hospitable florist received her very kindly and allowed her to spend the night in a room next to his garden. But the fragrant atmosphere of the

48

place was too good for the fisherwoman. She could not sleep for a long time. At last when she discovered that the sweet aroma of the flowers in the garden kept her awake, she sprinkled water on her empty basket of fish, placed it close to her nose, and immediately fell into a sound sleep. Such indeed is the power and influence of bad habits over all those who are addicted to them. They cannot enjoy the uplifting influence of the spiritual atmosphere.

RAMAKRISHNA

DAY 70   I S L A M

Jesus and the Fool

A certain fool was accompanying Jesus; he saw some bones in a hollow. He said, "O my companion, teach me that exalted name by which you make the dead alive. Teach it to me, in order that I may do a kindness—that by it I may give life to these bones."

Jesus answered, "Be silent; that business is beyond you. It is incongruous with your breathings and speech. For that business demands a breath purer than rain and more subtle in its action than are the angels. Lifetimes are required before the breath is purified, and one becomes thus a custodian of the treasury of the heavens. Supposing you indeed take this rod firmly in your hand, whence would your hand gain the cunning of Moses?"

The fool said, "If I am not one who should give utterance to such mysteries, then do you utter the name over the bones."

Jesus said, "O Lord, what mystery is this? What means the tendency of this fool toward such contention? Why is not this sick man solicitous about himself? Why has this lifeless carrion no care for life in himself? He leaves his own dead personality and seeks to restore an alien corpse."

God said, "He who is an alien to grace seeks and finds naught but disgrace and adversity: if thorny brambles grow, it is the requital of his sowing. He who sows the seeds of thorny brambles in the world—do not seek him in a rose garden. If he takes a rose in his hand, it becomes a thorn; if he goes toward a friend, that friend becomes a serpent. That miserable wretch is the

49

alchemy of snake-poison, in contrast to the alchemy of the pious man."

MASNAVI

The Cause of the Human Person

The good of civilization is also the good of the human person, the recognition of his rights and of his dignity, based ultimately on the fact that he is the image of God. Let no one deceive himself; the cause of religion and the cause of the human person are closely linked. They have the same enemies. The time has passed when a rationalism fatal to reason, which has prepared the way for all our misfortunes, could claim to defend the person and his autonomy *against* religion. Both against atheistic materialism and against an irrationalism drunk with inflicting domination and humiliation, an irrationalism which perverts the genuine instincts of human nature and makes of the political State a supreme idol and a Moloch, religion is the best defender of the person and of his freedom.

And finally if I am asked what I believe to be the reason for God's having permitted the religious divisions in mankind, and those heresies which "must be," according to Saint Paul—I should answer: For the education of mankind, and in order to prepare the way for final religious unity. Because on the one hand it is something above human powers to maintain purity and strength in the collective virtues of any natural community, unless it be within the particular hereditary bias of this earthly, sociologically closed social group. And on the other hand the common life of the church, the Kingdom of God, is that of a spiritual, supernatural, supra-racial, supra-national, supra-earthly community, open to all humanity as it is open to Deity and divine and deifying blood. Much suffering and many purifications throughout human history are necessary to extricate us from any restrictions and adulteration of spiritual unity brought about by fleshly unities.

JACQUES MARITAIN

Idolatry and Judgment

Certain philosophers once asked the elders at Rome, "If your God has no pleasure in idolatry, why does He not destroy the objects of it?" "And so He would," was the reply, "if only such objects were worshiped as the world does not stand in need of; but you idolators will worship the sun and moon, the stars and the constellations. Should He destroy the world because of the fools that are in it? No! The world goes on as it has done all the same, but they who abuse it will have to answer for their conduct. On your philosophy, when one steals a measure of wheat and sows it in his field, it should by rights produce no crop; nevertheless the world goes on as if no wrong had been done, and they who abuse it will one day smart for it."

AUODA ZARAH

Wisdom from Trees

Tzu Ch'i of Nan-poh was traveling on the Shang mountain when he saw a large tree which astonished him very much. A thousand chariot teams could have found shelter under its shade.

"What tree is this?" cried Tzu Ch'i. "Surely it must have unusually fine timber." Then, looking up, he saw that its branches were too crooked for rafters, while the trunk's irregular grain made it valueless for coffins. He tasted a leaf, but it took the skin off his lips, and its odor was so strong that it would make a man drunk for three days together.

"Ah!" said Tzu Ch'i. "This tree is good for nothing, and that is how it attained this size. A wise man might well follow its example."

CHUANG TZU

The Nine Incapabilities

The brother . . . in whom the intoxicants are destroyed, who has lived the life, who has done the task, who has laid low his burden, who has attained salvation, who has utterly destroyed the fetter of rebirth, who is emancipated by the true gnosis, he is incapable of perpetrating nine things:

1. He is incapable of deliberately depriving a living creature of life.

2. He is incapable of taking what is not given so that it constitutes theft.

3. He is incapable of sexual impurity.

4. He is incapable of deliberately telling lies.

5. He is incapable of laying up treasure for indulgence in worldly pleasure as he used to do in the life of the house.

6. He is incapable of taking a wrong course through partiality.

7. He is incapable of taking a wrong course through hate.

8. He is incapable of taking a wrong course through stupidity.

9. He is incapable of taking a wrong course through fear.

These nine things the *arahant* in whom the mental intoxicants are destroyed, who has lived the life, whose task is done, whose burden is laid low, who has attained salvation, who has utterly destroyed the fetter of becoming, who is emancipated by the true gnosis, is incapable of perpetrating.

PASADIKA SUTTANTA

Sharing the Vision of Salvation

A place was enclosed by means of a high wall. The men outside did not know what sort of place it was. Once four persons determined to find out what was inside by scaling the wall with a ladder. As soon as the first man ascended to the top of the wall, he laughed, "Ha, ha, ha!" and jumped in. The second also, as soon as he ascended, similarly laughed aloud and jumped in, and so did the third. When the fourth and last man got up to the top of the wall, he found stretched beneath him a large and beautiful garden containing pleasant groves and delicious fruits. Though strongly tempted to jump down and enjoy the scene, he resisted the temptation, and coming down the ladder, preached the glad tidings about the beautiful garden to all outsiders. The Brahman is like the walled garden. He who sees it forgets his own existence and with ecstatic joy rushes headlong unto it to attain to Moksha, or absolute freedom. Such are the holy men and liberated saints of the world. But the saviors of humanity are those who see God and, being at the same time anxious to share their happiness of divine vision with others, refuse the final liberation, and willingly undergo the troubles of rebirth in the world in order to teach and lead struggling humanity to its ultimate goal.

RAMAKRISHNA

DAY 76   ISLAM

Lying Against God

. . . And who does greater evil than he who forges
against God a lie? Those shall be presented
before their Lord, and the witnesses will say,
"Those are they who lied against their Lord."
Surely the curse of God shall rest upon the evildoers
who bar from God's way, desiring to make it
crooked; they disbelieve in the world to come;
they are unable to frustrate Him on earth
and they have no protectors, apart from God.
For them the chastisement shall be doubled;
they could not hear, neither did they see.
Those are they that have lost their souls, and
that they forged has gone astray from them;
they without doubt will be the greatest losers
    in the world to come.
But those who believe, and do righteous deeds,
and have humbled themselves unto their Lord—

they shall be the inhabitants of Paradise,
    therein dwelling forever.
The likeness of the two parties
is as the man blind and deaf, and the man who
sees and hears; are they equal in likeness?
    Will you not remember?

THE KORAN

DAY 77

JUDAISM-
CHRISTIANITY

The Return to Zion

The eyes of the blind shall be opened, and the ears of the deaf shall be unstopped. Then shall the lame man leap as an hart, and the tongue of the dumb sing: for in the wilderness shall waters break out, and streams in the desert. And the parched ground shall become a pool and the thirsty land springs of water; in the habitations of dragons, where each lay, shall be grass with reeds and rushes. And an highway shall be there, and a way, and it shall be called the way of holiness; the unclean shall not pass over it; but it shall be for those: the wayfaring men, though fools, shall not err therein. No lion shall be there, nor any ravenous beast shall go up thereon, it shall not be found there; but the redeemed shall walk there. And the ransomed of the Lord shall return, and come to Zion, with songs and everlasting joy upon their heads: they shall obtain joy and gladness, and sorrow and sighing shall flee away.

ISAIAH 35:5-10

DAY 78

CONFUCIANISM

Man's Nature Is Good

The disciple Kung-tu said, "The philosopher Kaou says, 'Man's nature is neither good nor bad.' Some say, 'Man's nature may be made to practice good, and it may be made to practice evil, and accordingly, under Wan and Wu, the people loved what was good, while under Yew and Le, they loved what was cruel.'

"Some say, 'The nature of some is good, and the nature of others is bad. . . .

"And now you say, 'The nature is good.' Then are all those wrong?"

Mencius said, "From the feelings proper to it, it is constituted for the practice of what is good. This is what I mean in saying that the nature is good.

"If men do what is not good, the blame cannot be imputed to their natural powers.

"The feeling of commiseration belongs to all men; so does that of shame and dislike, and that of reverence and respect, and that of approving and disapproving. The feeling of commiseration implies the principle of benevolence; that of shame and dislike, the principle of righteousness; that of reverence and respect, the principle of propriety; and that of approving and disapproving, the principle of knowledge. Benevolence, righteousness, propriety, and knowledge are not infused into us from without. We are certainly furnished with them. And a different view is simply from want of reflection. Hence it is said, 'Seek and you will find them. Neglect and you will lose them.' Men differ from one another in regard to them—some as much again as others, some five times as much, and some to an incalculable amount. It is because they cannot carry out fully their natural powers."

MENCIUS

DAY 79   STOICISM
Mutual Interdependence

Begin the morning by saying to thyself, I shall meet with the busybody, the ungrateful, arrogant, deceitful, envious, unsocial. All these things happen to them by reason of their ignorance of what is good and evil. But I who have seen the nature of the good that it is beautiful, and of the bad that it is ugly, and the nature of him who does wrong, that it is akin to me, not only of the same blood or seed, but that it participates in the same intelligence and the same portion of the divinity, I can neither be injured by any of them, for no one can fix on me what is ugly, nor can I be

55

angry with my kinsman, nor hate him. For we are made for co-operation, like feet, like hands, like eyelids, like the rows of the upper and lower teeth. To act against one another then is contrary to nature; and it is acting against one another to be vexed and to turn away.

MARCUS AURELIUS

The Right Use of the Present Life

The Lord commands every one of us, in all the actions of life, to regard his vocation. For he knows with what great inquietude the human mind is inflamed, with what desultory levity it is hurried hither and thither, and how insatiable is its ambition to grasp different things at once. Therefore, to prevent universal confusion being produced by our folly and temerity, he has appointed to all their particular duties in different spheres of life. And that no man might rashly transgress the limits prescribed, he has styled all such spheres of life *vocations* or *callings*. Every individual's life, therefore, is, as it were, a post assigned him by the Lord, that he may not wander about in uncertainty all his days. . . . It is not my design, however, to stay to enumerate examples. It is sufficient if we know that the principle and foundation of right conduct in every case is the vocation of the Lord, and that he who disregards it will never keep the right way in the duties of his station. He may sometimes, perhaps, achieve something apparently laudable. But however it may appear in the eyes of men, it will be rejected at the throne of God—besides which, there will be no consistency between the various parts of his life. Our life, therefore, will then be best regulated when it is directed to this work, since no one will be impelled by his own temerity to attempt more than is compatible with his calling, because he will know that it is unlawful to transgress the bounds assigned him. He that is in obscurity will lead a private life without discontent so as not to desert the station in which God has placed him. It will be no small alleviation of his cares, labors, troubles, and other burdens, when a man knows that in all these things he has God for his guide. The magistrate will execute his office with greater pleasure, the father of a family will confine himself to his duty with more satisfaction, and all in their respective spheres of life will bear and surmount the inconveniences, cares, disappointments, and anxieties which befall them when they shall be persuaded that every individual has his burden laid upon him by God. . . .

JOHN CALVIN

DAY 81   ISLAM
Cursing

Beware of cursing anything that God most high has created, whether animal or food or man himself. . . . The one who apprehends secrets is God most high; do not interfere between him and his servants. On the day of resurrection you will certainly not be asked, "Why did you not curse so-and-so? Why were you silent about him?" . . . But if you cursed anyone whom God created, you will have to give an account.

AL GHAZALI

DAY 82   TAOISM
Gain and Loss

When Chuang Tzu was wandering in the Tiao-ling park, he saw a strange bird which came from the south. Its wings were seven feet across. Its eyes were an inch in circumference. And it flew close past Chuang Tzu's head to alight in a chestnut grove. "What manner of bird is this?" cried Chuang Tzu. "With strong wings it does not fly away. With large eyes it does not see." So he picked up his skirts and strode toward it with his crossbow, anxious to get a shot. Just then he saw a cicada enjoying itself in the shade, forgetful of all else. And he saw a mantis spring and seize it, forgetting in the act its own body, which the strange bird immediately pounced upon and made its prey. And this it was which had caused the bird to forget its own nature. "Alas!" cried Chuang Tzu with a sigh. "How creatures injure one another. Loss follows the pursuit of gain."

So he laid aside his bow and went home, driven away by the park keeper who wanted to know what business he had there. For three months after this, Chuang Tzu did not leave the house.

CHUANG TZU

JUDAISM

Hatred of One's Neighbor

It is forbidden for an Israelite to hate his neighbor; for it is written: "Thou shalt not hate thy brother in thine heart." (Lev. 19:17) And we find that it was the hatred of the brothers for Joseph which brought our ancestors into the slavery of Egypt. . . . Our Rabbis have taught: "Thou shalt not hate thy brother." Perhaps by this might be understood: "Thou shalt not wound him, thou shalt not quarrel with him, thou shalt commit no outrage against him." It is for this reason that the prophet adds: "Thou shalt not hate thy brother in *thine heart;* in order to make clear that it is not permitted to carry hatred toward any one within one's self, even if no outward expression is given to it. As to the punishment which is foreseen for unjustified hatred, it is equal to that which is imposed for the three capital crimes, which are: idolatry, luxury, and murder. . . . Why did the first Temple fall? Because of idolatry, luxury, and murder. . . . And why did the second Temple fall, since we know that in its time the Torah was observed, good works were practiced, and the commandments were respected? It fell because of the unjustified hatreds which reigned then, from which it may be concluded that unjustified hatred is a sin as heavy as idolatry, luxury, and murder.

GAON ACHAI SHABCHA

HINDUISM

True Benevolence

The loftiest trees bend humbly to the ground
Beneath the teeming burden of their fruit;

High in the vernal sky the pregnant clouds
Suspend their stately course, and, hanging low,
Scatter their sparkling treasures o'er the earth:
And such is true benevolence; the good
Are never rendered arrogant by riches.

KALIDASA

DAY 85 ZOROASTRIANISM
Associations With Men

With enemies fight with equity. With a friend proceed with
the approval of friends. With a malicious man carry on no conflict,
and do not molest him in any way whatever. With a greedy man
you should not be a partner, and do not trust him with leadership.
With a slanderous man do not go to the door of kings. With an
ill-famed man form no connection. With an ignorant man you
should not become a confederate and associate. With a foolish
man make no dispute. With a drunken man do not walk on the
road. From an ill-natured man take no loan.

MENOG-I-KHRAD

DAY 86 LAMAISM
(TIBETAN BUDDHISM)
Aphorisms from the Tree of Wisdom

The root-principle of mankind is not to quarrel.
What would you do with wealth obtained by quarreling?
What would you do with wealth and life
Obtained by pride and suppression of good?

Real Truth is a virtue to the talented,
But a harmful thing to those without talent.
The water of the river is very free from impurity;
But, entering the ocean, it becomes undrinkable.

Let all hear this moral maxim,
And having heard it keep it well:
Whatever is not pleasing to yourself,
Do not that unto others.

SHE-RAB DONG-BU

DAY 87   ZOROASTRIANISM
The Treatment of Others

Him who is less than you, consider as an equal, and an equal
as a superior, and a greater than him as a chieftain, and a chieftain as a ruler.

MENOG-I-KHRAD

DAY 88   SIKHISM
The Worship of God

O servant of God the Inscrutable,
Cease to think of worldly occupations.
Become the dust of the feet of poor travelers; thus shall thy
  darwesh be accepted at God's door.
Make truth thy prayer, faith thy prayer-carpet; chasten desires,
  and subdue thy feelings.
Make thy body the mosque, thy conscience the Mulla, and the
  very pure God thy creed. . . .
Make the subjection of thy ten organs the rosary by which God
  is remembered in thy heart;
Good conduct and great restraint over thyself, thy circumcision.
Know thy heart that everything is for the moment.
Sports, banquets, and sodalities are all entanglements.
Kings, rulers, and nobles are perishable; God's gate alone is the
  stable place.
Let these be thy five most precious kinds of prayer: first, God's
  praises; second, patience;
Third, mildness; fourth, almsgiving;

60

Fifth, the five evil passions restrained in one place.
Make the knowledge that God is everywhere thy daily worship;
The abandonment of evil deeds the water-pot in thy hand;
The knowledge that there is but one God thy call to prayer; such
a Muezzin shall have an excellent reward.
What is honestly obtained eat thou as thy food;
Wash away thy filth in the river of thy heart. . . .
Make good works thy body, faith thy spouse,
And obedience to God thy pleasures and spectacles.
Purify what is impure, make God's presence thy Hadis; let a
complete body be the turban on thy head.

ARJAN

DAY 89   CHRISTIANITY
Counsels of Perfection

Ye have heard that it hath been said, An eye for an eye, and a
tooth for a tooth: But I say unto you, That ye resist not evil: but
whosoever shall smite thee on thy right cheek, turn to him the
other also. And if any man will sue thee at the law, and take away
thy coat, let him have thy cloke also. And whosoever shall compel
thee to go a mile, go with him twain. Give to him that asketh
thee, and from him that would borrow of thee, turn not thou
away. Ye have heard that it hath been said, Thou shalt love thy
neighbour, and hate thine enemy. But I say unto you, Love your
enemies, bless them that curse you, do good to them that hate
you, and pray for them which despitefully use you, and persecute
you; That ye may be the children of your Father which is in
heaven; for he maketh his sun to rise on the evil and on the good,
and sendeth rain on the just and on the unjust. For if ye love
them which love you, what reward have ye? do not even the
publicans the same? And if ye salute your brethren only, what do
ye more than others? do not even the publicans so? Be ye therefore perfect, even as your Father which is in heaven is perfect.

MATTHEW 5:38-48

No Absolute

If a man sleeps in a damp place, he gets lumbago and dies. But how about an eel? And living up in a tree is precarious and trying to the nerves—but how about monkeys? Of the man, the eel, and the monkey, whose habitat is absolutely the right one? Human beings feed on flesh, deer on grass, centipedes on snakes, owls and crows on mice. Of these four, whose is absolutely the right taste? Monkey mates with monkey, the buck with the doe; eels consort with fishes, while men admire Mao Ch'iang and Li Chi, at the sight of whom fishes plunge deep down in the water, birds soar high in the air, and deer hurry away. Yet who shall say which is the correct standard of beauty? In my opinion, the standard of human virtue, and of positive and negative, is so obscured that it is impossible actually to know it as such.

CHUANG TZU

The Immersion of the Heart

When I look upon chaste women of respectable families, I see in them the divine Mother arrayed in the garb of a chaste lady; and again, when I look upon the public women of the city, sitting in their verandas, arrayed in the garb of immorality and shamelessness, I see in them also the divine Mother sporting in a different way.

Man is like a pillowcase. The color of the one may be red, that of another blue, that of a third black, but all contain the same cotton. So it is with man—one is beautiful, another is ugly, a third holy, a fourth wicked, but the divine One dwells within them all.

God tells the thief to go and steal, and at the same time warns the householder against the thief.

If you fill an earthen vessel with water and set it apart upon a shelf, the water in it will dry up in a few days; but if you immerse the same vessel in water, it will remain filled as long as it is kept there. Even so is the case of your love for the Lord God. Fill and enrich your bosom with the love of God for a time and then employ yourself in other affairs, forgetting him all the while, and then you are sure to find within a short time that your heart has become poor and vacant and devoid of that precious love. But if you keep your heart immersed always in the ocean of divine love, your heart is sure to remain ever full to overflowing with the waters of the divine love.

RAMAKRISHNA

DAY 92   JUDAISM
The Community of Man

Rabbi Akiba said: "Beloved is man, for he was created in the image of God; but it was by a special love that it was made known to him that he was created in the image of God.

"Everything is foreseen, yet freedom of choice is given; and the world is judged by grace, yet all is according to the amount of work."

Ben Azzai said: "Despise not any man, and carp not at anything; for there is not a man that has not his hour, and there is not a thing that has not its place."

Hillel said: "If I am not for myself, who will be for me? And being for myself only, what am I? and if not now, when?

"Separate not thyself from the community. Trust not in thyself until the day of thy death. Judge not thy neighbor until thou art come into his place."

PIRKE ABOTH

DAY 93   ISLAM
The Evil in Ourselves

The Lion took the Hare with him: they ran together to the well and looked in.

63

The Lion saw his own image: from the water appeared the form
of a lion with a plump hare beside him.

No sooner did he espy his enemy than he left the Hare and
sprang into the well.

He fell into the pit which he had dug: his iniquity recoiled on
his own head.

O Reader, how many an evil that you see in others is but your
own nature reflected in them!

In them appears all that *you* are—your hypocrisy, iniquity, and
insolence.

You do not see clearly the evil in yourself, else you would hate
yourself with all your soul.

Like the Lion who sprang at his image in the water, you are only
hurting yourself, O foolish man.

When you reach the bottom of the well of your own nature,
then you will know the wickedness in *you*.

JALALU'L-DIN RUMI

DAY 94   JUDAISM-
                                          CHRISTIANITY

The Temple of the Lord

Thus saith the Lord of hosts, the God of Israel, Amend your
ways and your doings, and I will cause you to dwell in this place.

Trust ye not in lying words, saying, The temple of the Lord,
the temple of the Lord, the temple of the Lord, are these. For if
ye thoroughly amend your ways and your doings; if ye thoroughly
execute judgment between a man and his neighbour; if ye oppress not the stranger, the fatherless, and the widow, and shed
not innocent blood in this place, neither walk after other gods to
your hurt; then will I cause you to dwell in this place, in the land
that I gave to your fathers, for ever and ever.

Behold, ye trust in lying words, that cannot profit. Will ye
steal, murder, and commit adultery, and swear falsely, and burn
incense unto Baal, and walk after other gods whom ye know
not? . . .

Seest thou not what they do in the cities of Judah and in the streets of Jerusalem? The children gather wood, and the fathers kindle the fire, and the women knead their dough to make cakes to the queen of heaven, and to pour out drink-offerings unto other gods, that they may provoke me to anger. Do they provoke me to anger? saith the Lord: do they not provoke themselves to the confusion of their own faces?

Therefore thus saith the Lord God; Behold, mine anger and my fury shall be poured out upon this place, upon man, and upon beast, and upon the trees of the field, and upon the fruit of the ground; and it shall burn, and shall not be quenched.

JEREMIAH 7:3-9, 17-20

DAY 95   CONFUCIANISM
Resistance to Wrong Commands

Tseng Tzu said: "I have heard all that you said about parental love, filial love, reverence to elders, how to treat parents every day, and how to please them by making oneself known for good conduct; and now I will venture to ask you whether it is filial that a son should obey every command of his father, whether right or wrong?"

"What do you say?—what do you say?" replied Confucius. "Once upon a time there was a certain emperor who would have lost his empire through wickedness except that he had seven good ministers who often checked his illegal actions by strong protests; there was also a feudal baron who would have lost his feudal estate through wantonness, but for the fact that he had five good men who often made strong remonstrances to him; and there was also a statesman who would have brought frightful calamity upon his family, but for the fact that he had three good servants who often strongly advised him not to do what he ought not.

"If a man has a good friend to resist him in doing bad actions, he will have his reputation preserved; so if a father has a son to resist his wrong commands, he will be saved from committing serious faults.

"When a command is wrong, a son should resist his father, and a minister should resist his august master.

"The maxim is, 'Resist when wrongly commanded.' Hence how can he be called filial who obeys his father when he is commanded to do wrong?"

THE HSIAO KING

DAY 96   HINDUISM
The Price of Knowledge

How can a man love knowledge yet repose?
If you wish to be learned, then abandon ease,
Either give up your knowledge or your rest.

MAHABHARATA

DAY 97   AMERICAN INDIAN
We Die Forever

One time Old Man said to Old Woman, "People will never die."
"Oh!" said Old Woman, "that will never do; because, if people
live always, there will be too many people in the world."
"Well," said Old Man, "we do not want to die forever. We shall
die for four days and then come to life again."
"Oh, no!" said Old Woman, "it will be better to die forever, so
that we shall be sorry for each other."
"Well," said Old Man, "we will decide this way. We will throw
a buffalo-chip into the water: if it sinks, we will die forever;
if it floats, we shall live again."
"Well," said Old Woman, "throw it in."
Now, Old Woman had great power, and she caused the chip to
turn into a stone, so it sank.
So when we die, we die forever.

BLACKFOOT INDIAN MYTH

DAY 98   CHRISTIANITY
Faith and History

According to the Christian faith all finite and historical existence points to a ground and an end beyond itself. This divine end

66

and ground is paradoxically defined as having a double relation to history. God judges the world because there are violations of the law of life on every level of human achievement. God "saves" the world because he has resources of mercy beyond his judgment. But mercy cannot express itself without taking justice seriously. Thus God is pictured as being able to be merciful only by taking the consequences of his judgment upon and into himself. These paradoxes of the Christian faith have sometimes been stated in terms of a wooden literalism that has made them offensive to human intelligence. But it is well to remember that they are a "stumbling block" and "foolishness" even when stated profoundly. The reason for this is that all men would like to believe that they have the power within themselves to complete their lives and their history. But this is exactly what all men lack.

A faith that is able to transcend the catastrophes of history must therefore be able to define both the possibilities of human creativity in history and the limits of human possibilities. It must also be able to clarify the fact that the evils of fanaticism, conflict, imperialism, and tyranny have their source in man's ambition to overleap his limitations and to seek unconditioned power, virtue, and security for his existence.

For this reason historical catastrophe seems to be nothing but chaos, which drives men to despair without the profundities of the Christian faith. And Christian faith becomes vapid and sentimental in periods of stability and peace. It recovers its own profoundest insights precisely in those periods of social chaos when all simpler interpretations of life break down and force men to seek for a profounder interpretation of existence.

REINHOLD NIEBUHR

DAY 99   ISLAM

True Piety

It is not piety, that you turn your faces
    to the East and to the West.
        True piety is this:
to believe in God, and the Last Day,

the angels, the Book, and the Prophets,
to give of one's substance, however cherished,
    to kinsmen, and orphans,
the needy, the traveller, beggars,
    and to ransom the slave,
to perform the prayer, to pay the alms.
And they who fulfil their covenant, . . .
    and endure with fortitude
    misfortune, hardship and peril,
these are they who are true in their faith,
    these are the truly godfearing.

THE KORAN

Trammels of Mortality

When Lao Tzu died, Ch'in Shih went to mourn. He uttered three yells and departed.

A disciple asked him, "Were you not our Master's friend?"

"I was," replied Ch'in Shih.

"And if so, do you consider that a sufficient expression of grief at his loss?" added the disciple.

"I do," said Ch'in Shih. "I had believed him to be the man of all men, but now I know that he was not. When I went in to mourn, I found old persons weeping as if for their children, young ones wailing as if for their mothers. And for him to have gained the attachment of those people in this way, he too must have uttered words which should not have been spoken and dropped tears which should not have been shed, thus violating eternal principles, increasing the sum of human emotion, and forgetting the source from which his own life was received. The ancients called such emotions the trammels of mortality. The Master came, because it was his time to be born; he went, because it was his time to die. For those who accept the phenomenon of birth and death in this sense, lamentation and sorrow have no place. The ancients spoke of death as of God cutting down a man suspended in the air. The fuel is consumed, but the fire may be transmitted, and we know not that it comes to an end."

CHUANG TZU

DAY 101

JUDAISM-
CHRISTIANITY

The Lord Is My Light and My Salvation

The Lord is my light and my salvation; whom shall I fear? The Lord is the strength of my life; of whom shall I be afraid? When the wicked, even mine enemies and my foes, came upon me to eat up my flesh, they stumbled and fell. Though an host should encamp against me, my heart shall not fear: though war should rise against me, in this will I be confident. One thing have I desired of the Lord, that will I seek after; that I may dwell in the house of the Lord all the days of my life, to behold the beauty of the Lord, and to inquire in his temple. For in the time of trouble he shall hide me in his pavilion: in the secret of his tabernacle shall he hide me; he shall set me up upon a rock. And now shall mine head be lifted up above mine enemies round about me: therefore will I offer in his tabernacle sacrifices of joy; I will sing, yea, I will sing praises unto the Lord. Hear, O Lord, when I cry with my voice: have mercy also upon me, and answer me. When thou saidst, Seek ye my face; my heart said unto thee, Thy face, Lord, will I seek. Hide not thy face far from me; put not thy servant away in anger; thou hast been my help; leave me not, neither forsake me, O God of my salvation. When my father and my mother forsake me, then the Lord will take me up. Teach me thy way, O Lord, and lead me in a plain path, because of mine enemies. Deliver me not over unto the will of mine enemies: for false witnesses are risen up against me, and such as breathe out cruelty. I had fainted, unless I had believed to see the goodness of the Lord in the land of the living. Wait on the Lord: be of good courage, and he shall strengthen thine heart: wait, I say, on the Lord.

PSALM 27

The Worth of Life

To save one human life is better than to build a seven-storied
   pagoda.

Better bestow blessings nearby than burn incense afar.

The ancients did not see the moon of the present; the present
   moon did once shine upon the ancients.

Beauty does not delude man to folly; it is man who deludes himself to folly.

A mind enlightened is heaven; a mind darkened is hell.

Cultivate in this life merits of the life of the future.

He who sees through superficialities regards death and life as so
   much sorrow while lingering, and so much freedom after
   quitting.

The mind is really nothingness. Leave defamations and frowns
   alone. Both are easy to tolerate.

[Some people possess] the mouth of a Buddha but the heart of a
   serpent.

The human mind makes mischiefs, like a monkey; human consciousness gallops like a horse.

CHINESE BUDDHIST PROVERBS

Drowning in Talk

Confucius said, "The common man often gets in trouble because
of his love for the water [literally "gets drowned" in it]; the
gentleman often gets into trouble because of his love for talking;
and the great man often gets into trouble because of his love for
the people. All of them get submerged in what they come close
to or are familiar with. Water seems so familiar to the people, but
it easily drowns them because it is a thing that seems so easy to
approach and yet is dangerous to get too near to. Talking easily
leads one into trouble because when you talk, you use so many

words, and it is easy to let them out of your mouth, but difficult to take them back. The people often get one into trouble because they are mean and not open-minded; you can respect them, but you must not insult or offend them. Therefore the gentleman must be very careful."

ANALECTS

DAY 104 JUDAISM

Daily Sustenance

The scholars of Rabbi Simon ben Jochai once asked him: "Why did not the Lord give to Israel enough manna to last them for a year at one time, instead of meting it out daily?"

The Rabbi replied: "I will answer you with a parable. There was once a king who had a son to whom he gave a certain yearly allowance, paying the entire sum for his year's support on one appointed day. It soon happened that this day, on which the allowance was due, was the only day in the year when the father saw his son. So the king changed his plan, and each day gave his son his maintenance for that day only, and then the son visited his father with the return of each day's sun.

"So it was with Israel; each father of a family, dependent for his support and the support of his family upon the manna provided each day by God's bounty, naturally had his mind devoted to the Great Giver and Sustainer of life."

RABBINICAL ANA

DAY 105 HINDUISM

The Ways of Wise Men

He who excites the wrath of foes and then
Sits down inactively, is like a man
Who kindles withered grass and then lies near
While a strong wind is blowing from beyond.

Soft words, intended to alleviate,
Often foment the wrath of one enraged,
Like drops of water poured on burning butter.

The foolish undertake a trifling act
And soon desist, discouraged; wiser men
Engage in mighty works and persevere.

The undertaking of a careless man
Succeeds not, though he use the right expedients;
A clever hunter, though well placed in ambush,
Kills not his quarry if he fall asleep.

SISUPALA BADHA

DAY 106   CHRISTIANITY
Putting on the Life of Christ

Now, wherever a man has been made a partaker of the divine
nature, in him is fulfilled the best and noblest life, and the
worthiest in God's eyes, that has been or can be. And of that
eternal love which loves Goodness as Goodness and for the sake
of Goodness, a true, noble, Christlike life is so greatly beloved
that it will never be forsaken or cast off. Where a man has tasted
this life, it is impossible for him ever to part with it, were he to
live until the Judgment Day. And though he must die a thousand
deaths, and though all the sufferings that ever befell all creatures
could be heaped upon him, he would rather undergo them all
than fall away from this excellent life; and if he could exchange
it for an angel's life, he would not.

This is our answer to the question, "If a man, by putting on
Christ's life, can get nothing more than he has already, and serve
no end, what good will it do him? This life is not chosen in order
to serve any end, to get anything by it, but for love of its noble-
ness, and because God loves and esteems it so greatly: And
whoever says that he has had enough of it and may now lay it
aside has never tasted or known it; for he who has truly felt or
tasted it can never give it up again. And he who has put on the
life of Christ, seeking to win or deserve anything thereby, has
taken it up as a hireling and not for love, and is altogether without it. For he who does not take it up for love has none of it at
all; he may dream indeed that he has put it on, but he is de-

72

ceived. Christ did not lead such a life as His for the sake of reward, but out of love; and love makes such a life light and takes away all its hardships so that it becomes sweet and is gladly endured. But to him who has not put it on from love, but has done so, as he dreams, for the sake of reward, it is utterly bitter and a weariness, and he would gladly be quit of it. And it is a sure token of a hireling that he wishes his work were at an end. But he who truly loves it is not offended at its toil or suffering, or the length of time it lasts. . . .

THEOLOGIA GERMANICA

DAY 107   BUDDHISM
The Deed Bears Fruit

A man may spoil another, just so far
As it may serve his ends, but when he's spoiled
By others he, despoiled, spoils yet again.
So long as evil's fruit is not matured,
The fool doth fancy "Now's the hour, the chance!"
But when the deed bears fruit, he fareth ill.
The slayer gets a slayer in his turn;
The conqueror gets one who conquers him;
Th' abuser wins abuse, th' annoyer fret.
Thus by evolution of the deed
A man who spoils is spoiled in his turn.

SAMYUTTA NIKAYA

DAY 108   HINDUISM
The Marks of a Good Man

Wise men rest not on destiny alone,
Nor yet on manly effort, but on both.

Weak persons gain their object when allied
With strong associates; the rivulet
Reaches the ocean by the river's aid.

73

A good man's intellect is piercing, yet
Inflicts no wound; his actions are deliberate,
Yet bold; his heart is warm, but never burns;
His speech is eloquent, yet ever true.

SISUPALA BADHA

DAY 109   CHRISTIANITY
Accusing Another Before God

There was once a criminal who had stolen some money, among
the rest a hundred dollar note. He wished to change this, and
therefore he offered it to another criminal who lived in the same
house. He accepted the note, went into the next room as if to get
change, came out again, innocently greeted the waiting visitor as
if he now saw him for the first time: in short, he defrauded him
out of the hundred dollar note. The first man became so enraged
at this, that in his indignation he reported the matter to the legal
authorities, telling how shamefully he had been swindled. The
other was naturally arrested, and arraigned as an imposter. Alas,
in the trial, the first question the magistrate asked was how the
accuser had obtained the money. So there were two cases. Of
course the first man was wholly right in thinking that he
had been swindled; he would now be the honest man, the good
citizen, who reported the matter to the authorities in order to
secure his rights. Oh, but the judge does not deal with matters
in his private capacity, or with an isolated case one chooses to
bring before him; nor does he always give the case the turn which
the accuser and informer gives: the magistrate looks deeper into
the matter. And so with the God-relationship. As soon as you ac-
cuse another man before God, then there are immediately found to
be two cases; just when you come to lay information about the
other man, God begins to consider how you are connected with
the case.

SØREN KIERKEGAARD

74

The Rules of Propriety

Respectfulness, without the rules of propriety, becomes laborious bustle; carefulness, without the rules of propriety, becomes timidity; boldness, without the rules of propriety, becomes insubordination; straightforwardness, without the rules of propriety, becomes rudeness.

I have not seen one who loves virtue as he loves beauty.

A youth is to be regarded with respect. How do we know that his future will not be equal to our present? If he reaches the age of forty or fifty, and has not made himself heard of, then indeed he will not be worth being regarded with respect.

Hold faithfulness and sincerity as first principles. Have no friends not equal to yourself. When you have faults, do not fear to abandon them.

ANALECTS

The Honor Due to Parents

"Three friends," said the Rabbis, "has man. God, his father, and his mother. He who honors his parents honors God."

Rabbi Judah said, "Known and revealed are the ways of man. A mother coaxes a child with kind words and gentle ways, gaining honor and affection; therefore, the Bible says, 'Honor thy father,' before 'Honor thy mother.' But in regard to fearing, as the father is the preceptor of the child, teaching it the law, the Bible says, 'Every man shall fear his mother,' before the word 'father.'"

Rabbi Ulah was once asked, "How extended should be this honor due to parents?"

He replied: "Listen, and I will tell you how thoroughly it was observed by a heathen, Damah, the son of Nethina. He was a diamond merchant, and the sages desired to purchase from him a

75

jewel for the ephod of the high priest. When they reached his house, they found that the key of the safe in which the diamond was kept was in the possession of Damah's father, who was sleeping. The son absolutely refused to wake his father to obtain the key, even when the sages in their impatience offered him a much larger sum for the jewel than he had demanded. And further, when his father awoke, and he delivered the diamond to the purchasers, and they offered him the larger sum which they had named, he took from it his first price, returning the balance to them, with the words, 'I will not profit by the honor of my father.' "

RABBINICAL ANA

The Night Journey

. . . And slay not your children for fear of poverty;
    We will provide for you and them;
surely the slaying of them is a grievous sin.
    And approach not fornication;
surely it is an indecency, and evil as a way.
    And slay not the soul God has
forbidden, except by right. Whosoever is slain
    unjustly, We have appointed to
his next-of-kin authority, but let him not exceed
    in slaying; he shall be helped.
And do not approach the property of the orphan
save in the fairest manner, until he is of age.
And fulfil the covenant; surely the covenant
    shall be questioned of.
And fill up the measure when you measure, and
weigh with the straight balance; that is better
    and fairer in the issue.
And pursue not that thou hast no knowledge of;
the hearing, the sight, the heart—all of those
    shall be questioned of.
And walk not in the earth exultantly; certainly

thou wilt never tear the earth open, nor attain
  the mountains in height.
All of that—the wickedness of it is hateful
  in the sight of thy Lord.

THE KORAN

DAY 113 TAOISM

The Intrinsic Value of Creatures

Mr. T'ien of the Ch'i State was holding an ancestral banquet
in his hall, to which a thousand guests were bidden. As he sat in
their midst, many came up to him with presents of fish and game.
Eyeing them approvingly, he exclaimed with unction: "How
generous is Almighty God to man! He makes the five kinds of
grain to grow, and creates the finny and feathered tribes, especially
for our benefit." All Mr. T'ien's guests applauded this sentiment
to the echo.

But the twelve-year-old son of a Mr. Pao, regardless of seniority,
came forward and said, "You are wrong, my lord. All the living
creatures of the universe stand in the same category as ourselves,
and one is of no greater intrinsic value than another. It is only
by reason of size, strength, or cunning that some particular species
gains the mastery, or that one preys upon another. None of them
is produced in order to subserve the use of others. Man catches and
eats those that are fit for food, but how can it be maintained that
God creates these expressly for man's use? Mosquitoes and gnats
suck man's blood, and tigers and wolves devour his flesh; but we
do not therefore assert that God created man expressly for the
benefit of mosquitoes and gnats, or to provide food for tigers and
wolves."

LIEH TZU

DAY 114 SIKHISM

The True One Blesses

Pilgrimage and penance and free-will giving
Gain for one no single grain of merit,

77

Unless one harken and his heart be loving,
Cleansed within by a meditative bath.
All good is thine, no single virtue have I,
And without it what avails devotion?
By word of mouth the brahmans utter blessing,
While the True One blesses with sincere desire.

What indeed of sun-course, moon-phase, week-day,
What of months and seasons and their varied forms?
Pandits fail to gauge them, though Purans inform them,
And qadis do not know the times of the Koran,
Neither does the yogi know the times and seasons,
He alone doth know them by whom they have been made.
Who then am I to know, relate and praise,
If not to use the clever words of others?
Saith Nanak of the Lord, his name and will are great
And pride of self meets in the end dishonor.

THE JAPJI

Of God and the World

Never yet has God existed
And never will he do so;
Yet he will survive the world
As, alone, he was before it.

God knows no distinctions,
All to him have equal worth;
He holds as much in common
With the fly as with you.

Having much is not being rich.
He is a wealthy man
Who, without grief, can bear
The loss of all he owns.

Not for its own sake falls the rain,
Nor idly shines the sun;
You too were made for others,
Not for yourself alone.

What you wish your neighbor
You ask God to give you;
Not wishing him to prosper
Is asking death for yourself.

ANGELUS SILESIUS

DAY 116   BUDDHISM

Mankind Revolves by Deeds

By deeds one is a farmer and by deeds
An artisan, by deeds a trader too;
By deeds one is a servant and a thief,
By deeds a soldier and a celebrant,
And even so a rajah is by deeds.
'Tis thus in truth the wise perceive the deed.
Seers of the origin by way of cause,
Men expert in the result of deeds. The world
Revolves by deeds, mankind revolves by deeds:
As pin holds fast the rolling chariot's wheel,
So beings are in bondage held by deeds.

SUTTA NIPATA

DAY 117   ISLAM

Uprooting Bad Habits

A softspoken but insensitive man planted a bramble bush in
the middle of the road. Passers-by reproached him and repeatedly
told him to dig it up, but he did not do so.

The bramble bush kept on growing and people's feet were
bloodied and their clothes torn by its sharp thorns. Finally the
governor ordered him to dig it up, and the man replied: "Yes, I
will dig it up someday."

For a long time he kept on promising to do it tomorrow, while the bramble bush continued to grow, becoming firm and robust. Then one day the governor said to him: "O promise breaker, come forward and do my business; don't creep back." The man replied: "O uncle, the days are between us." The governor said: "Hurry, do not defer what you owe me. You keep saying 'tomorrow,' but there is something that you must learn. Every day that time brings, that evil tree grows younger, gains strength and becomes greener and fresher by the minute. And every day, you who are supposed to dig it up are getting older and more helpless. You had better be quick and not waste any more time. Dig it up now while you still have some strength left!"

Consider the bramble bush as any bad habit of yours. For the thorns of a bad habit will often wound your feet. You have often been wounded by your evil nature—you have absolutely no sense at all. If you are heedless of others wounded by your evil nature, you are at least not heedless of your own wounds.

MASNAVI

JUDAISM-
                                                CHRISTIANITY

God Is a Witness

Love uprightness, you who judge the land,
Think of the Lord with goodness,
And seek him with sincerity of heart.
For he is found by those who do not try him,
And is manifested to those who do not disbelieve him.
For crooked reasonings separate from God,
And when his power is tested, it exposes fools.
For wisdom cannot enter a deceitful soul,
Or live in a body in debt to sin.
For the holy spirit of instruction will flee from deceit,
And will rise and leave at unwise reasoning,
And be put to confusion at the approach of wrong.
For wisdom is a kindly spirit,
And will not acquit a blasphemer of what he says,

For God is a witness of his heart,
And a truthful observer of his mind,
And a hearer of his tongue.
For the spirit of the Lord fills the world,
And that which embraces all things knows all that is said.
Therefore no one who utters what is wrong will go unobserved,
Nor will justice, in its investigation, pass him by.
For there will be an inquiry into the designs of the ungodly,
And the sound of his words will reach the Lord,
To convict him of his transgressions;
For a jealous ear hears everything,
And the sound of grumbling is not hidden.

THE WISDOM OF SOLOMON I:I-IO

DAY 119   TAOISM
Knowledge and Fulfilment

He who knows what God is, and who knows what man is, has
attained. Knowing what God is, he knows that he himself pro-
ceeded therefrom. Knowing what man is, he rests in the knowledge of the known, waiting for the knowledge of the unknown.
Working out one's allotted span, and not perishing in mid-career,
this is the fulness of knowledge.

God is a principle which exists by virtue of its own intrin-
sicality, and operates spontaneously, without self-manifesta-
tion. . . .

Herein, however, there is a flaw. Knowledge is dependent upon
fulfilment. And as this fulfilment is uncertain, how can it be
known that my divine is not really human, my human really
divine?

CHUANG TZU

DAY 120   JUDAISM
All That God Does Is Done Well

Rabbi Akiba was once traveling through the country, and he
had with him an ass, a rooster, and a lamp.

At nightfall he reached a village where he sought shelter for the night without success.

"All that God does is done well," said the Rabbi, and proceeding toward the forest he resolved to pass the night there. He lit his lamp, but the wind extinguished it. "All that God does is done well," he said. The ass and the rooster were devoured by wild beasts; yet still he said no more than "All that God does is done well."

Next day he learned that a troop of the enemy's soldiers had passed through the forest that night. If the ass had brayed, if the rooster had crowed, or if the soldiers had seen his light he would surely have met with death, therefore he said again, "All that God does is done well."

RABBINICAL ANA

DAY 121   CONFUCIANISM
Firmness in Energy

Tsze-lu asked about energy.

The Master said, "Do you mean the energy of the South, the energy of the North, or the energy which you should cultivate yourself?

"To show forbearance and gentleness in teaching others, and not to revenge unreasonable conduct—this is the energy of Southern regions, and the good man makes it his study.

"To lie under arms, and meet death without regret—this is the energy of Northern regions, and the forceful make it their study.

"Therefore, the superior man cultivates a friendly harmony, without being weak. How firm is he in his energy! He stands erect in the middle, without inclining to either side. How firm he is in his energy! When good principles prevail in the government of his country, he does not change from what he was in retirement. How firm is he in his energy! When bad principles prevail in the country, he maintains his course to death without changing. How firm is he in his energy!"

THE DOCTRINE OF THE MEAN

Work with Hope

Cast thy bread upon the waters; for thou shalt find it after many days. Give a portion to seven, yea, even unto eight; for thou knowest not what evil shall be upon the earth. If the clouds be full of rain, they empty themselves upon the earth; and if a tree fall toward the south, or toward the north, in the place where the tree falleth, there shall it be. He that observeth the wind shall not sow; and he that regardeth the clouds shall not reap. As thou knowest not what is the way of the wind, nor how the bones do grow in the womb of her that is with child; even so thou knowest not the work of God who doeth all. In the morning sow thy seed, and in the evening withhold not thy hand; for thou knowest not which shall prosper, whether this or that, or whether they both shall be alike good. Truly the light is sweet, and a pleasant thing it is for the eyes to behold the sun. Yea, if a man live many years, let him rejoice in them all; but let him remember the days of darkness, for they shall be many. All that cometh is vanity.

ECCLESIASTES 11:1-8

Death Our Fellow Traveler

Wherever we walk, Death marches at our side;
Wherever we sit, Death seats himself beside us;
However far we journey, Death continues
Our fellow traveler and goes with us home.
Men take delight in each returning dawn,
And with admiring gaze, behold the glow
Of sunset. Every season, as it comes,
Fills them with gladness, yet they never think
That each recurring season, every day,
Fragment by fragment bears their life away.

As drifting logs of wood may chance to meet
On ocean's waters, surging to and fro,
And having met, drift once again apart;
So fleeting is a man's association
With wife and children, relatives and wealth,
So surely must a time of parting come.

RAMAYANA

DAY 124   CHRISTIANITY
Fruit in Due Season

Lord, I confess this morning I remembered my breakfast, but
forgot my prayers. And as I have returned no praise, so Thou
mightst justly have afforded me no protection. Yet Thou hast
carefully kept me to the middle of this day, intrusted me with a
new debt before I have paid the old score. It is now noon, too
late for a morning, too soon for an evening sacrifice. My corrupt
heart prompts me to put off my prayers till night; but I know
it too well, or rather too ill, to trust it. I fear, if till night I defer
them, at night I shall forget them. Be pleased, therefore, now
to accept them. Lord, let not a few hours the later make a
breach; especially seeing (be it spoken not to excuse my negli-
gence, but to implore Thy pardon) a thousand years in Thy
sight are but as yesterday. I promise hereafter, by Thy assistance,
to bring forth fruit in due season. See how I am ashamed the
sun should shine on me, who now newly start in the race of my
devotions, when he, like a giant, hath run more than half his
course in the heavens.

THOMAS FULLER

DAY 125   ISLAM
Reconciling Brothers

If two parties of the believers fight,
put things right between them; then
if one of them is insolent against

84

the other, fight the insolent one
till it reverts to God's commandment.
If it reverts, set things right between
them equitably, and be just. Surely
    God loves the just.
The believers indeed are brothers;
so set things right between your
two brothers, and fear God; haply so
    you will find mercy.

THE KORAN

DAY 126

JUDAISM-
CHRISTIANITY

Trust in the Lord

Thus saith the Lord; Cursed be the man that trusteth in man and maketh flesh his arm, and whose heart departeth from the Lord. For he shall be like the heath in the desert, and shall not see when good cometh; but shall inhabit the parched places in the wilderness, in a salt land and not inhabited. Blessed is the man that trusteth in the Lord, and whose hope the Lord is. For he shall be as a tree planted by the waters, and that spreadeth out her roots by the river, and shall not see when heat cometh, but her leaf shall be green; and shall not be careful in the year of drought, neither shall cease from yielding fruit. The heart is deceitful above all things and desperately wicked: who can know it?

JEREMIAH 17:5-9

DAY 127

BUDDHISM

The Heart of a Mother

It is said that a woman carrying her child on her hip went to the tank to bathe, and leaving him lying upon her clothes entered the water. Thereupon straightway an Ogress, seeing the boy and desiring to eat him, took the form of a woman and standing by him called to the mother, "What a pretty child this is! May I suckle him?" The mother agreed, and the Ogress, taking him up, gave him some milk and then ran away with him. When the mother seized her she put on a bold face and claimed the child as her own. Now it chanced that, as they wrangled over the child, they passed by the Judgment Hall; and the Bodhisat, hearing their quarrel, sent for them and asked them the cause of the dispute. As he looked upon the Ogress he perceived that her eyes were red as Olinda seeds and did not blink, and knowing her to be an Ogress, he asked, "Will you be content to abide by my decision?" They agreed, and he bade the attendants draw a line upon the ground, and lay the child upon it exactly in the middle. He then told the Ogress to grasp the boy's arms, and the mother to grasp his legs, and both to pull, until one prevailed, and pulled him over the line. "Whoso wins," he declared, "shall become the possessor of the child!"

They began to try and the child to scream with pain; whereat the mother, yearning over him, let go her son and stood lamenting. The Bodhisat turned to those who stood by and asked them, "Whose heart is pitiful to children, the heart of a mother or the heart of a stranger?" And they answered, "O wise man! it is the heart of a mother that is tender." . . . So the mother took her child in her arms and went out saying, "Long may you live, O master!"

UMMAGGA JATAKA

DAY 128   TAOISM
On Treating a Bird as a Bird

Sun Hsiu went away, and Pien Tzu went in and sat down. Shortly afterwards, he looked up to heaven and sighed; whereupon a disciple asked him what was the matter.

"When Hsiu was here just now," answered Pien Tzu, "I spoke to him of the virtue of the perfect man. I fear lest he be startled and so driven on to doubt."

"No, Sir," answered the disciple. "If he was right and you were wrong, wrong will never drive right into doubt. If, on the other hand, he was wrong and you were right, he brought his doubt with him, and you are not responsible."

"Not so," said Pien Tzu. "Of old, when a bird alighted outside the capital of Lu, the prince was delighted, and killed an ox to feed it, and had the Chiu Shao played to entertain it. The bird, however, was timid and dazed, and dared not to eat or drink. This was treating the bird like oneself. But to treat a bird as a bird would treat a bird, you must put it to roost in a deep forest, and let it swim in river or lake and feed at its ease on the plain. Now Sun Hsiu is a man of small understanding, and for me to speak to him of the perfect man is like setting a mouse to ride in a coach, or a band of music to play to a quail. How should he not be startled?"

CHUANG TZU

DAY 129   JUDAISM

Luck

Rava said, "Life, children, and competency do not depend on one's merit, but on luck; for instance, Rabbah and Rav Chasda were both righteous rabbis. The one prayed for rain and it came, and the other did likewise with the like result. Yet Rav Chasda lived ninety-two years and Rabbah only forty. Rav Chasda, moreover, had sixty weddings in his family during his lifetime, whereas Rabbah had sixty serious illnesses in his during the short period of his life. At the house of the former even the dogs refused to eat bread made of the finest wheat flour, whereas the family of the latter were content to eat rough bread of barley and could not always obtain it." Rava also added, "For these three things I prayed to Heaven, of which two were and one was not granted to me. I prayed for the wisdom of Rav Hunna and for the riches of Rav Chasda, and both these were granted to me; but the humility and meekness of Rabbah, the son of Rav Hunna, for which I also prayed, was not granted."

MOED KATON

Honor From God, Not Man

Moreover, when the Lord sent me forth into the world, He forbade me to put off my hat to any, high or low. And I was required to thee and thou all men and women, without any respect to rich or poor, great or small. And as I travelled up and down I was not to bid people good-morrow or good-evening, neither might I bow or scrape with my leg to any one; and this made the sects and professions to rage. But the Lord's power carried me over all to his glory, and many came to be turned to God in a little time; for the heavenly day of the Lord sprang from on high and brake forth apace, by the light of which many came to see where they were.

But, oh! the rage that then was in the priests, magistrates, professors, and people of all sorts, but especially in priests and professors; for though thou to a single person was according to their own learning, their accidence, and grammar rules, and according to the Bible, yet they could not bear to hear it; and the hat-honour, because I could not put off my hat to them, it set them all into a rage. But the Lord showed me that it was an honour below, which He would lay in the dust and stain it—an honour which proud flesh looked for, but sought not the honour which came from God only. That it was an honour invented by men in the fall and in the alienation from God, who were offended if it were not given them, and yet would be looked upon themselves as saints, church-members, and great Christians; but Christ saith, How can ye believe, who receive honour one of another, and seek not the honour that cometh from God only? and I, saith Christ, receive not honour of men. Showing that men have an honour which men will receive and give, but Christ will have none of it. This is the honour which Christ will not receive and which must be laid in the dust.

GEORGE FOX

The Sacred Tortoise

Chuang Tzu was fishing in the P'u when the Prince of Ch'u sent two high officials to ask him to take charge of the administration of the Ch'u State.

Chuang Tzu went on fishing and, without turning his head, said: "I have heard that in Ch'u there is a sacred tortoise which has been dead now some three thousand years, and that the Prince keeps this tortoise carefully enclosed in a chest on the altar of his ancestral temple. Now, would this tortoise rather be dead and have its remains venerated, or be alive and wagging its tail in the mud?"

"It would rather be alive," replied the two officials, "and wagging its tail in the mud."

"Begone!" cried Chuang Tzu. "I too will wag my tail in the mud."

CHUANG TZU

Who Created This World?

A Min once asked Rabbi Akiba, "Who created this world?" "The Holy One—blessed be He!" was the reply. "Give me positive proof of this," begged the other. "Come tomorrow," answered the Rabbi. On coming the next day, the Rabbi asked, "What are you dressed in?" "In a garment," was the reply. "Who made it?" asked the Rabbi. "A weaver," said the other. "I don't believe you," said the Rabbi. "Give me positive proof." "I need not demonstrate this," said the Min. "It stands to reason that a weaver made it." "And so you may know that God created the world," observed the Rabbi. When the Min had departed, the Rabbi's disciples asked him, "What is proof positive?" He said, "My children, as a house implies a builder, and a garment a weaver, and a door a carpenter, so likewise the existence of the world implies that the Holy One—blessed be He!—created it."

MIDRASH TEROMAH

DAY 133   HINDUISM

The Leveling of Distinctions

By anger, fear, and avarice deluded,
Men do not strive to understand themselves,
Nor ever gain self-knowledge. One is proud
Of rank, and plumes himself upon his birth,
Contemning those of low degree; another
Boasts of his riches, and disdains the poor;
Another vaunts his learning and, despising
Men of less wisdom, calls them fools; a fourth
Piquing himself upon his rectitude,
Is quick to censure other peoples' faults.
But when the high and low, the rich and poor,
The wise and foolish, worthy and unworthy,
Are borne to their last resting place—the grave—
When all their troubles end in that last sleep,
And of their earthly bodies naught remains
But fleshless skeletons—can living men
Mark differences between them, or perceive
Distinctions, in the dust, of birth or form?
Since all are, therefore, leveled by the grave,
And all must sleep together in the earth—
Why, foolish mortals, do you wrong each other?

MAHABHARATA

DAY 134   ISLAM

The Stinters

In the Name of God, the Merciful, the Compassionate

Woe to the stinters
who, when they measure against the people, take full measure

but, when they measure for them or weigh for them, do skimp.
Do those not think that they shall be raised up
unto a mighty day
a day when mankind shall stand before the Lord of all Being?

THE KORAN

DAY 135   CONFUCIANISM
Superior and Inferior Men

Men of loftier mind manifest themselves in their equitable dealings; small-minded men in their going after gain.

When you meet with men of worth, think how you may attain to their level; when you see others of an opposite character, look within, and examine yourself.

A son, in ministering to his parents, may (on occasion) offer gentle remonstrances; when he sees that their will is not to heed such, he should nevertheless still continue to show them reverent respect, never obstinacy; and if he has to suffer, let him do so without murmuring.

While the parents are still living, he should not wander far; or, if a wanderer, he should at least have some fixed address.

If for three years he does not veer from the principles of his father, he may be called a dutiful son.

A son should not ignore the years of his parents. On the one hand, they may be a matter for rejoicing (that they have been so many), and on the other, for apprehension (that so few remain).

People in olden times were loth to speak out, fearing the disgrace of not being themselves as good as their words.

Those who keep within restraints are seldom losers.

To be slow to speak but prompt to act is the desire of the superior man.

Virtue dwells not alone: she must have neighbors.

ANALECTS

Evenness in Vigor

Sona Kolivisa, a merchant's son, received his going forth in the Lord's presence, he received ordination. Because of his great output of vigor while pacing up and down, his feet split and the place for pacing up and down in became stained with blood as though cattle had been slaughtered there. As the venerable Sona was meditating in private he thought: "The Lord's disciples, of whom I am one, dwell putting forth vigor; but even so my mind is not freed from the outflows with no [further] clinging, and moreover there are my family's possessions. Suppose I were to return to the low life, enjoy the possessions and do good?"

The Lord knew by mind the thoughts in the venerable Sona's mind. He approached him and said: "Sona, formerly when you were a householder were you clever at the lute's stringed music?"

"Yes, Lord."

"When the strings of the lute were too taut, was it tuneful and fit for playing?"

"Certainly not, Lord."

"And when they were too slack, was the lute tuneful and fit for playing?"

"No, Lord."

"But when the strings were neither too taut nor too slack but were keyed to an even pitch, was your lute tuneful and fit for playing?"

"Yes, Lord."

"Even so, Sona, does too much output of vigor conduce to restlessness and too feeble a vigor to slothfulness. Therefore, Sona, determine on evenness in vigor."

VINAYA PITAKA

Injustice Dries Up the Heart

A cheerful face is a sign of a happy heart,
But it takes painstaking thought to compose proverbs!
How happy is the man who makes no slip with his mouth,
And is not stabbed with sorrow for his sins!
Happy is the man whose heart does not condemn him,
And who has not given up hope.
Wealth does not become a niggardly man,
And what use is money to an envious man?
The man who withholds from himself amasses for others,
And others will enjoy his goods.
If a man is evil to himself, to whom will he be good?
For he will not take any pleasure in his own money.
There is nobody worse than the man who is grudging to himself,
And that is the penalty of his wickedness.
If he does any good, he does it through forgetfulness,
And shows his wickedness in the end.
He is a wicked man who has an envious eye,
Turning away his face, and pretending not to see human souls.
A covetous man's eye is never satisfied with what he gets,
And wicked injustice dries up the heart.
An evil eye begrudges bread,
And is in want of it at his own table.
My child, if you have any means, provide well for yourself,
And make suitable offerings to the Lord.
Remember that death will not delay,
And the agreement of Hades has not been shown to you.
Treat your friend well before you die,
And reach out and give to him as much as your strength permits.

THE WISDOM OF SIRACH 13:26-14:13

Brothers Are Best

The flowers of the cherry tree—
Are they not gorgeously displayed?
Of all the men in the world
There are none equal to brothers.

Brothers may quarrel inside the walls,
But they will oppose insult from without,
When friends, however good they may be,
Will not afford help.

When death and disorder are past,
And there are tranquility and rest,
Although they have brothers,
Some reckon them not equal to friends.

Loving union with wife and children
Is like the music of lutes;
But it is the accord of brothers
Which makes the harmony and happiness lasting.

For the ordering of your family,
For your joy in your wife and children,
Examine this and study it;
Will you not find that it is truly so?

THE SHIH KING

God and Mammon

Lay not up for yourselves treasures upon earth, where moth
and rust doth corrupt, and where thieves break through and steal.
But lay up for yourselves treasures in heaven, where neither moth
nor rust doth corrupt, and where thieves do not break through
nor steal; for where your treasure is, there will your heart be

also. The light of the body is the eye: if therefore thine eye be single, thy whole body shall be full of light. But if thine eye be evil, thy whole body shall be full of darkness. If therefore the light that is in thee be darkness, how great is that darkness. No man can serve two masters: for either he will hate the one, and love the other; or else he will hold to the one, and despise the other. Ye cannot serve God and mammon.

MATTHEW 6:19-24

Knowing and Feeling

Chuang Tzu and Hui Tzu had strolled onto the bridge over the Hao, when the former observed: "See how the minnows are darting about! That is the pleasure of fishes."

"Not being a fish yourself," said Hui Tzu, "how can you possibly know in what consists the pleasure of fishes?"

"And not being I," retorted Chuang Tzu, "how can you know that I do not know?"

"If I, not being you, cannot know what you know," urged Hui Tzu, "it follows that you, not being a fish, cannot know in what consists the pleasure of fishes."

"Let us go back," said Chuang Tzu, "to your original question. You asked me how I knew in what consists the pleasure of fishes. Your very question shows that you knew I knew. I knew it from my own feelings on this bridge."

CHUANG TZU

Deep River

The source of life is God. The mystic applies this to human life when he says that there is in man an uncreated element; or in the Book of Job where it is written that his mark is in their foreheads. In the last analysis the mood of reverence that should characterize all men's dealings with each other finds its basis here. The demand to treat all human beings as ends in themselves, or the moral imperative that issues in respect for personality, finds its profound inspiration here. To deal with men on any other basis, to treat them as if there were not vibrant and vital in each one the very life of the very God, is the great blasphemy; it is the judgment that is leveled with such relentless severity on modern man. "Thou hast made us for thyself and our souls are restless till they find their rest in thee," says Augustine. Life is like a river.

> Deep River, my home is over Jordan—
> Deep River, I want to cross over into camp ground.

HOWARD THURMAN

DAY 142   BUDDHISM
Variations in the Teaching of the Dhamma

A village headman spoke thus to the Lord:

"Is a Tathagata compassionate towards all living breathing creatures?"

"Yes, headman," answered the Lord.

"But does the Lord teach Dhamma in full to some, but not likewise to others?"

"Now, what do you think, headman? Suppose a farmer had three fields, one excellent, one mediocre, and one poor with bad soil. When he wanted to sow the seed, which field would he sow first?

"He would sow the excellent one, then the mediocre one. When he had done that, he might or might not sow the poor one with the bad soil. And why? Because it might do, if only for cattle fodder.

"In the same way, headman, my monks and nuns are like the excellent field. It is to these that I teach Dhamma that is lovely at the beginning, lovely in the middle and lovely at the ending, with the spirit and the letter, and to whom I make known the Brahma-faring completely fulfilled, utterly pure. And why? It is these that dwell with me for light, me for shelter, me for stronghold, me for refuge.

96

"Then my men and women lay followers are like the mediocre field. To these too I teach Dhamma . . . and make known the Brahma-faring completely fulfilled, utterly pure. For they dwell with me for light, me for shelter, me for stronghold, me for refuge.

"Then recluses, Brahmins and wanderers of other sects than mine are like the poor field with the bad soil. To these too I teach Dhamma . . . and make known the Brahma-faring completely fulfilled, utterly pure. And why? Because if they were to understand even a single sentence, that would be a happiness and a blessing for them for a long time."

SAMYUTTA NIKAYA

DAY 143   CONFUCIANISM
The Rule Is Not Changed for the Stupid

Kung-sun Ch'ou said, "Lofty are your principles and admirable, but to learn them may well be likened to ascending the heavens— something which cannot be reached. Why not adapt your teachings so as to cause learners to consider them attainable, and so daily exert themselves?"

Mencius said, "A great artificer does not, for the sake of a stupid workman, alter or do away with the marking line. Yi did not, for the sake of a stupid archer, change his rule for drawing the bow.

"The superior man draws the bow, but does not discharge the arrow. The whole thing seems to leap before the learner. Such is his standing exactly in the middle of the right path. Those who are able, follow him."

MENCIUS

DAY 144   JUDAISM
The Equality of Creatures

I am a creature of God, and my neighbor is also His creature; my work is in the city, and his in the field; I rise early to my work, and he rises early to his. As he cannot excel in my work, so I cannot excel in his work. But perhaps you say, I do great things,

and he does small things. We have learnt it matters not whether
a man does much or little, if only he direct his heart to Heaven.

BERAKOTH

DAY 145   ISLAM
God's True Measure

O men, a similitude is struck; so
give your ear to it. Surely those upon
whom you call, apart from God, shall never
create a fly, though they banded together
to do it; and if a fly should rob them
of aught, they would never rescue it from him.
Feeble indeed alike are the seeker
    and the sought!
They measure not God with His true measure; surely God is
    All-strong, All-mighty.

God chooses of the angels Messengers
and of mankind; surely God is
    All-hearing, All-seeing.
He knows whatsoever is before them
and behind them, and unto God all
    matters are returned.

THE KORAN

DAY 146   JUDAISM-
                                        CHRISTIANITY
Swords Into Ploughshares

For the law shall go forth of Zion, and the word of the Lord
from Jerusalem. And he shall judge among many people, and re-
buke strong nations afar off; and they shall beat their swords into
ploughshares, and their spears into pruning hooks; nation shall
not lift up a sword against nation, neither shall they learn war
any more.

But they shall sit every man under his vine and under his fig tree; and none shall make them afraid: for the mouth of the Lord of hosts hath spoken it.

For all people will walk every one in the name of his god, and we will walk in the name of the Lord our God for ever and ever.

In that day, saith the Lord, will I assemble her that halteth, and I will gather her that is driven out, and her that I have afflicted; And I will make her that halted a remnant, and her that was cast far off a strong nation: and the Lord shall reign over them in mount Zion from henceforth, even for ever.

MICAH 4:2-7

DAY 147   HINDUISM

True Happiness

The man who every sacred science knows,
Yet has not strength to keep in check the foes
That rise within him, mars his Fortune's fame
And brings her by his feebleness to shame.

Success is like a lovely woman, wooed
By many men, but folded in the arms
Of him alone who free from over-zeal
Piously persists and calmly perseveres.

The noble-minded dedicate themselves
To the promotion of the happiness
Of others—even of those who injure them.
True happiness consists in making happy.

Youth's glories are as transient as the shadow
Of an autumnal cloud; and sensual joys,
Though pleasant at the moment, end in pain.

Riches and pleasure are the root of evil;
Hold them not dear, encourage not their growth;
They are aggressors hard to be subdued,
Destroyers of all knowledge and of truth.

99

The friendship of the bad is like the shade
Of some precipitous bank with crumbling sides,
Which falling buries him who sits beneath.

KIRATARJUNIYA

DAY 148

JUDAISM-
CHRISTIANITY

The Humility of the Wise

He that correcteth a scoffer getteth to himself reviling;
And he that reproveth a wicked man getteth himself a blot.
Reprove not a scoffer, lest he hate thee.
Reprove a wise man, and he will love thee.
Give instruction to a wise man, and he will be yet wiser;
Teach a righteous man, and he will increase in learning.

PROVERBS 9:7-9

DAY 149

JUDAISM

Brotherly Love

Love one another from the heart; and if a man sins against you, speak peaceably to him, and in your soul do not hold guile; and if he repents and confesses, forgive him. But if he denies it, do not get into a passion with him, lest catching the poison from you he takes to swearing and thus sins doubly. Do not let another man hear your secrets when engaged in legal strife, lest he come to hate you and become your enemy, and commit a great sin against you; for he often addresses you guilefully or busies himself about you with wicked intent. And though he denies it and yet has a sense of shame when reproved, do not reprove him. For he who denies may repent so as not to wrong you again; yes, he may also honor you, and fear and be at peace with you. But if he is shameless and persists in his wrongdoing, forgive him from the heart, and leave the avenging to God.

THE TESTAMENTS OF THE TWELVE PATRIARCHS

100

The Parable of the Raft

"Monks, I will teach you Dhamma—the Parable of the Raft—for crossing over, not for retaining. Listen to it, attend carefully, and I will speak.

"A man going along a highroad might see a great stretch of water, the hither bank dangerous and frightening, the farther bank secure, not frightening. But if there is no boat for crossing by or a bridge across for going from the not-beyond to the beyond, he might think: 'If I were to collect sticks, grass, branches, foliage and to tie a raft, then, depending on the raft and striving with my hands and feet, I might cross over safely to the beyond.' If he carried out his purpose, then, crossed over, gone beyond, it might occur to him: 'Now, this raft has been very useful to me. Depending on it and striving with my hands and feet, I have crossed over safely to the beyond. Suppose now, having put this raft on my head or lifted it on to my shoulder, I should proceed as I desire?' Now, monks, in doing this is that man doing what should be done with that raft?"

"No, Lord."

"But, monks, it might occur to him after he has crossed over and gone beyond: 'Now, this raft has been very useful to me. Depending on it and striving with my hands and feet, I have crossed over safely to the beyond. Suppose now, having beached this raft on the dry ground or having submerged it in the water, I should proceed as I desire?' In doing this, monks, that man would be doing what should be done with that raft. Even so is the Parable of the Raft Dhamma taught by me for crossing over, not for retaining. You, monks, by understanding the Parable of the Raft, should get rid even of [wholesome] mental states, all the more of unwholesome ones."

MAJJHIMA NIKAYA

Beware the Rich Man

Do not lift a load that is too heavy for you,
And do not associate with a man stronger or richer than you are.
What relation can an earthen pot have with a kettle?
The kettle knocks against it, and it is broken in pieces.
When a rich man does a wrong, he adds a threat;
When a poor man suffers a wrong, he must beg pardon.
If you can be useful, he makes you work for him,
And if you are in want, he abandons you.
As long as you have anything, he will live with you,
And will strip you bare, but he will feel no distress.
If he needs you, he will deceive you,
And smile upon you, and raise your hopes.
He will speak you fair and say, "Is there anything you need?"
He will shame you with his food,
Until he has impoverished you again and again,
And finally he will mock you.
Afterward when he sees you he will pass you by,
And shake his head at you.
Take care not to be misled,
And humbled through your own folly.
When a leading man invites you, be retiring,
And he will invite you all the more.
Do not press upon him, or you may be pushed away;
But do not stand too far off, or you may be forgotten.
Do not aim to speak to him as an equal,
But do not believe all he says;
For he will test you with much conversation,
And will examine you with a smile.

                    THE WISDOM OF SIRACH 13:2-11

Nine Tests of the Superior Man

The heart of man is more dangerous than mountains and rivers, more difficult to understand than Heaven itself. Heaven has its periods of spring, summer, autumn, winter, daytime and night. Man has an impenetrable exterior, and his motives are inscrutable. Thus some men appear to be retiring when they are really forward. Others have abilities, yet appear to be worthless. Others are compliant, yet gain their ends. Others take a firm stand, yet yield the point. Others go slow, yet advance quickly. Those who fly to duty toward their neighbor as though thirsting after it, drop it as though it were something hot. Thus the loyalty of the superior man is tested by employing him at a distance; his respectfulness, by employing him near at hand; his ability, by troublesome missions; his knowledge, by unexpected questions; his trustworthiness, by specification of time limits; his integrity, by entrusting him with money; his fidelity, by dangerous tasks; his decorum, by filling him with wine; his morality, by placing him in disreputable surroundings. Under the application of these nine tests, the inferior man stands revealed.

CHUANG TZU

Substitutes for God

The likeness of those who have taken
to them protectors, apart from God,
is as the likeness of the spider that takes
to itself a house; and surely the frailest
of houses is the house of the spider,
    did they but know.
God knows whatever thing they call upon
apart from Him; He is the All-mighty,
    the All-wise.

And those similitudes—We strike them
for the people, but none understands them
    save those who know.
God created the heavens and the earth
with the truth; surely in that is a sign
    to the believers.

Recite what has been revealed to thee
of the Book, and perform the prayer;
prayer forbids indecency and dishonour.
God's remembrance is greater; and God knows
    the things you work.

THE KORAN

CHRISTIANITY

DAY 154

Lukewarmness

Rather than hold on to the name of Christian lukewarmly, it doubtless would be better, for it would be a sign of life, if some people in our time were to admit bluntly to themselves that they could wish that Christianity never had come into the world or that they themselves had never become Christians. But let the admission be made without scorn and mockery and wrath. What is the use of that? One can well have reverence for that which one cannot compel oneself to accept. Christ himself says that He was attracted to the young man who nevertheless could not make up his mind to give all his possessions to the poor. The young man did not become a Christian, and yet Christ "loved" him. So then, better frank sincerity than lukewarmness. For Christianity is a fine belief to die in, the only true comfort, and the moment of death is the appropriate situation for Christianity. Perhaps it is for this reason that even the lukewarm will not give it up; for just as one deposits something in a burial society so as to be able when one's time comes to defray the costs, so does one keep Christianity treasured up until the last: one is a Christian, but becomes such only at the moment of death.

SØREN KIERKEGAARD

104

The Consequences of Behavior

As a goldsmith, taking a piece of gold, turns it into another, newer, and more beautiful form, so does this self, after having thrown off this body and dispelled all ignorance, make unto himself another, newer, and more beautiful shape . . . like that of Brahman. . . .

According as he acts, and according as he behaves, so will he be—a man of good acts will become good, a man of bad acts, bad. He becomes pure by pure deeds, bad by bad deeds. . . .

They who know the life of life, the eye of the eye, the ear of the ear, the mind of the mind—they have comprehended the ancient, primeval Brahman.

BRIHADARANYAKA UPANISHAD

The Fellowship of All Men

A branch cut off from the adjacent branch must of necessity be cut off from the whole tree also. So too a man when he is separated from another man has fallen off from the whole social community. Now as to a branch, another cuts it off, but a man by his own act separates himself from his neighbour when he hates him and turns away from him, and he does not know that he has at the same time cut himself off from the whole social system. Yet he has this privilege certainly from Zeus who framed society, for it is in our power to grow again to that which is near to us, and again to become a part which helps to make up the whole. However, if it often happens, this kind of separation, it makes it difficult for that which detaches itself to be brought to unity and to be restored to its former condition. Finally, the branch, which from the first grew together with the tree, and has continued to have one life with it, is not like that which after being cut off is then ingrafted, for this is something like what the gardeners

105

mean when they say that it grows with the rest of the tree, but that it has not the same mind with it.

As those who try to stand in thy way when thou art proceeding according to right reason, will not be able to turn thee aside from thy proper action, so neither let them drive thee from thy benevolent feelings towards them, but be on thy guard equally in both matters, not only in the matter of steady judgement and action, but also in the matter of gentleness towards those who try to hinder or otherwise trouble thee. For this also is a weakness, to be vexed at them, as well as to be diverted from thy course of action and to give way through fear; for both are equally deserters from their post, the man who does it through fear, and the man who is alienated from him who is by nature a kinsman and a friend.

MARCUS AURELIUS

Self-Deceit

You have spent all your life in the belief that you are wholly devoted to others, and never self-seeking. Nothing so feeds self-conceit as this sort of internal testimony that one is quite free from self-love, and always generously devoted to one's neighbours. But all this devotion which seems to be for others is really to yourself. Your self-love reaches the point of perpetual self-congratulation that you are free from it; all your sensitiveness is lest you might not be fully satisfied with self: this is at the root of all your scruples. You may prove it by your indifference to the faults of others; if you thought of nothing save God and his glory, you would be as keen and sensitive to others' losses as to your own. But it is the "I" which makes you so keen and sensitive. You want God as well as man to be always satisfied with you, and you want to be satisfied with yourself in all your dealings with God.

So pray turn your scruples upon this useless search after self-satisfaction in doing right.

FRANÇOIS DE FÉNELON

CONFUCIANISM
How the Sound of Music Reflects What Is Within

When the mind is moved to sorrow, the sound is sharp and fading away; when it is moved to pleasure, the sound is slow and gentle; when it is moved to joy, the sound is exclamatory and soon disappears; when it is moved to anger, the sound is coarse and fierce; when it is moved to reverence, the sound is straightforward, with an indication of humility; when it is moved to love, the sound is harmonious and soft. These six peculiarities of sound are not the nature of the voice; they indicate the impressions produced by external things. On this account the ancient kings were watchful to the things by which the mind was affected.

THE BOOK OF CEREMONIAL RITES

DAY 159 CHRISTIANITY
True Worship Is Holiness of Life

The true interior worship is the rectitude and perfection of the life of the interior man, by which God is honored above all. Every cause, in fact, is honored by the effect it produces; now there is no effect more noble than man, whose perfection will honor God in the proportion of its greatness, so that this perfection itself being in the proportion of the sanctity of life, it follows that the principal honor rendered to God is the good and perfect life of a man. Consequently, the true integral worship of God consists in the life and acts of the perfect man, and in the offering up to God of that life and its acts.

SAVONAROLA

DAY 160 HINDUISM
Foresight and Conscience

Reflect that health is transient, death impends,
Never in thy day of youthful strength do aught

To grieve thy conscience, lest when weakness comes,
And thou art on a bed of sickness laid,
Fear and remorse augment thy sufferings.

MAHABHARATA

BUDDHISM

The Root of Lust

A tree, as long as its root is firm and safe, although cut down, still survives and produces fruit. Likewise, unless the remnants of lust are destroyed and uprooted, a man must return again and again to receive sorrow. The monkey, away from the tree, first of all enjoys release, and then returns again to its bondage. Such is the case with men; they escape from hell and then return to it. Longing thoughts are like the ever-flowing waters of a river; giving way to the free enjoyment of indolence and luxury, the mind —like a savage dog—seeks for continued indulgence, and the man himself becomes clouded and unable to see the truth. Every thought flowing in the same channel—then lusts bind a man as with strong rattan bonds. The wise man alone is able rightly to distinguish the truth; he is able to cut off the very root and source of his lustful thoughts. A man by self-indulgence becomes sleek and shining, his thoughts increase like the sprouting tendril, the depth of lust cannot be fathomed; from this proceeds the ever-increasing succession of old age and continual death.

DHAMMAPADA

DAY 162   JUDAISM-
CHRISTIANITY

The Example of the Ant

Go to the ant, thou sluggard;
Consider her ways, and be wise:
Which having no chief, overseer, or ruler,
Provideth her bread in the summer,

And gathereth her food in the harvest.
How long wilt thou sleep, O sluggard?
When wilt thou arise out of thy sleep?
Yet a little sleep, a little slumber.
A little folding of the hands to sleep:
So shall thy poverty come as a robber,
And thy want as an armed man.

PROVERBS 6:6-11

DAY 163   JUDAISM

The Marks of a Wise Man

There are seven traits in a wise man:
He does not speak in the presence of one wiser than himself;
He does not interrupt when a colleague speaks;
He does not rush out with a rejoinder;
He asks questions that are relevant, and gives answers that are
logical;
He deals with first things first and last things last;
He readily admits when he does not know about a matter;
He acknowledges the truth.
The opposites of these traits mark the boorish man.

PIRKE ABOTH

DAY 164   TAOISM

Nature Can Do No Wrong

A son must go wherever his parents bid him. Nature is no other than a man's parents. If she bid me die quickly, and I demur, then I am an unfilial son. She can do me no wrong. Tao gives me this form, this toil in manhood, this repose in old age, this rest in death. And surely that which is such a kind arbiter of my life is the best arbiter of my death.

Suppose that the boiling metal in a smelting-pot were to bubble up and say: "Make of me an Excalibur"; I think the caster would reject that metal as uncanny. And if a sinner like myself were

109

to say to God: "Make of me a man, make of me a man"; I think he too would reject me as uncanny. The universe is the smelting-pot, and God is the caster. I shall go wherever I am sent, to wake unconscious of the past, as a man wakes from a dreamless sleep.

CHUANG TZU

Bodily Austerities

We will not, of course, rule out for ourselves or for others, the practice, or at least the spirit, also of bodily austerities. The spirit, and even some mild amount of the actual practice, of such austerities is indeed an integral constituent of all virile religion: the man who laughs at the plank bed and the discipline is a shallow fool. Indeed some souls are, undoubtedly, called to more than the minimum indicated, and only find their full peace and persuasiveness in some such bodily asceticism. Thus there was a Sacred Heart nun . . . who dearly loved and anxiously watched over one of the pupils of a convent school, a beautiful young woman. This young woman, soon after leaving the school, took to an evil life and became a wealthy man's mistress. The nun knew well how unavailing would be, in this case, any direct appeal to the girl's religion or conscience. So she wrote to the girl that she was sure the girl loved her and wished her to live for many a year. Well, she merely wanted the girl to know that on every day during which this her immoral life should last, she, the nun, would scourge herself till her feet stood in a pool of her own blood. That she had already carried out this plan daily since she knew of the girl's condition; and that nothing could or would stop her but the girl's own written announcement that she had left the man. The days went by. At last the girl wrote. The nun had gained her point. . . .

BARON FRIEDRICH VON HÜGEL

The Backbiter

In the Name of God, the Merciful, the Compassionate
    Woe unto every backbiter, slanderer,
  who has gathered riches and counted them over
  thinking his riches have made him immortal!

No indeed; he shall be thrust into the Crusher;
and what shall teach thee what is the Crusher?
    The Fire of God kindled
    roaring over the hearts
    covered down upon them,
    in columns outstretched.

THE KORAN

Aphorisms on Folly and Wisdom

A proverb on the lips of a fool will be refused
For he will not utter it at the proper time.
One man is kept from sinning through poverty,
So his conscience does not prick him when he goes to rest.
Another loses his own life from sheer embarrassment,
And destroys it by his senseless expression.
Another out of embarrassment makes promises to his friend,
And so makes him his enemy for nothing.
A lie is a bad blot in a man;
It is continually found on the lips of the ignorant.
A thief is better than a habitual liar,
But they are both doomed to destruction.
Dishonor is habitual with a liar,
And his shame attends him continually.

THE WISDOM OF SIRACH 20:20-26

The Foundation of Love From All

From love of lust comes sorrow, from lust comes fear; where there is no lust, or no ground for lust, what sorrow, what fear can there be? From pleasure comes sorrow, from pleasure comes fear; where there is no ground for pleasure, what grief or fear can there be? From covetousness comes sorrow, from greed comes fear; where one is free from covetousness, there can be no sorrow or fear. But to be greedy to fulfill perfectly the requirements of the Law—to be truthful in everything, or to be perfectly truthful, to be modest in everything, to conduct his own business according to what is right—this is to lay a foundation of love from all. The idea of pleasure not yet produced, his thoughts and words composed, his mind unaffected by any bewilderment of love, he indeed shall mount above or cut off the Stream.

DHAMMAPADA

Overcoming Men

Conquer a man who never gives by gifts;
Subdue untruthful men by truthfulness;
Vanquish an angry man by gentleness;
And overcome the evil man by goodness.

MAHABHARATA

Friendship's True Touchstone

A friend, the sight of whom is to the eyes
A balm—who is the heart's delight—who shares
Our joys and sorrows—is a treasure rare.
But other friendly persons who are ready

To share in our prosperity, abound.
Friendship's true touchstone is adversity.

HITOPADESA

CONFUCIANISM

The Attainment of Sincerity

To be fond of learning is to be near to knowledge. To practice with vigor is to be near to magnanimity. To possess the feeling of shame is to be near to energy.

He who knows these three things, knows how to cultivate his own character. Knowing how to cultivate his own character, he knows how to govern other men. Knowing how to govern other men, he knows how to govern the Empire with all its States and families. . . .

Sincerity is the way of Heaven. The attainment of sincerity is the way of men. He who possesses sincerity is he who arrives at what is right without an effort, and apprehends without the exercise of thought—he is the sage who naturally and easily embodies the right way. He who attains to sincerity is he who chooses what is good, and firmly holds it fast.

Requisites to this attainment are the extensive study of what is good, accurate inquiry about it, careful reflection on it, its clear discrimination, and its earnest practice.

THE DOCTRINE OF THE MEAN

JUDAISM

God Speaks in Silence

When God gave the Law, no bird sang or flew, no ox bellowed, the angels did not fly, the Seraphim ceased from saying, "Holy, holy," the sea was calm, no creature spoke; the world was silent and still, and the divine voice said: "I am the Lord thy God. . . ." If you wonder at this, think of Elijah: when he came to Mount Carmel, and summoned all the priests of Baal, and said to them, "Cry aloud, for he is a god," God caused all the world to

be still and those above and those below were silent, and the
world was, as it were, empty and void, as if no creature existed, as
it says, "There was no voice nor any answer." For if anyone had
spoken, the priests would have said, "Baal has answered us." So,
at Sinai, God made the whole world silent, so that all the creatures should know that there is no god beside Him, and so He
spoke: "I am the Lord, thy God," and so too, in the days to come,
He will say, "I, and I alone, am He that comforts you."

EXOD. R., YITRO

DAY 173 TAOISM

On Death

When Chuang Tzu was about to die, his disciples expressed a
wish to give him a splendid funeral. But Chuang Tzu said, "With
heaven and earth for my coffin and shell; with the sun, moon, and
stars as my burial regalia; and with all creation to escort me to
the grave, are not my funeral paraphernalia ready to hand?"

"We fear," argued the disciples, "lest the carrion kite should
eat the body of our Master"; to which Chuang Tzu replied,
"Above ground I shall be food for kites; below I shall be food for
mole-crickets and ants. Why rob one to feed the other?"

CHUANG TZU

DAY 174 GREEK

God and Justice

God, as the old tradition declares, holding in His hand the beginning, middle, and end of all that is, travels according to His
nature in a straight line towards the accomplishment of His end.
Justice always accompanies Him, and is the punisher of those who
fall short of the divine law. To justice he who would be happy
holds fast, and follows in her company with all humility and order; but he who is lifted up with pride, or elated by wealth or
rank or beauty, who is young and foolish, and has a soul hot with
insolence, and thinks that he has no need of any guide or ruler,

but he is able himself to be the guide of others, he, I say, is left deserted of God; and being thus deserted, he takes to him others who are like himself, and dances about, throwing all things into confusion, and many think that he is a great man; but in a short time he pays the penalty which justice cannot but approve, and is utterly destroyed, and his family and city with him.

PLATO, *Laws*

DAY 175   CHRISTIANITY

Follow Me

Then said Jesus unto his disciples, If any man will come after me, let him deny himself, and take up his cross, and follow me.

For whosoever will save his life shall lose it: and whosoever will lose his life for my sake shall find it. For what is a man profited, if he shall gain the whole world, and lose his own soul? or what shall a man give in exchange for his soul? For the Son of man shall come in the glory of his Father with his angels; and then he shall reward every man according to his works. Verily, I say unto you, There be some standing here, which shall not taste of death, till they see the Son of man coming in his kingdom.

MATTHEW 16:24-28

DAY 176   TAOISM

The Power of Calm Concentration

Ch'ing, the chief carpenter, was carving wood into a stand for hanging musical instruments. When finished, the work appeared to those who saw it as though of supernatural execution. And the Prince of Lu asked him, "What mystery is there in your art?"

"No mystery, your Highness," replied Ch'ing; "and yet there is something.

"When I am about to make such a stand, I guard against any diminution of my vital power. I first reduce my mind to absolute quiescence. Three days in this condition, and I become oblivious of any reward to be gained. Five days, and I become oblivious of

115

any fame to be acquired. Seven days, and I become unconscious of my four limbs and my physical frame. Then, with no thought of the Court present to my mind, my skill becomes concentrated and all disturbing elements from without are gone. I enter some mountain forest. I search for a suitable tree. It contains the form required, which is afterwards elaborated. I see the stand in my mind's eye, and then set to work. Otherwise, there is nothing. I bring my own natural capacity into relation with that of the wood. What was suspected to be of supernatural execution in my work was due solely to this."

CHUANG TZU

The Transience of Earthly Joys

In this decaying body, made of bones,
Skin, tendons, membranes, muscles, blood, saliva,
Full of putrescence and impurity,
What relish can there be for true enjoyment?
In this weak body, ever liable
To wrath, ambition, avarice, illusion,
To fear, grief, envy, hatred, separation
From those we hold most dear, association
With those we hate; continually exposed
To hunger, thirst, disease, decrepitude,
Emaciation, growth, decline, and death,
What relish can there be for true enjoyment?
The universe is tending to decay,
Grass, trees, and animals spring up and die.
But what are they? Earth's mighty men are gone,
Leaving their joys and glories; they have passed
Out of this world into the realm of spirits.
But what are they? Beings greater still than these,
Gods, demigods, and demons, all have gone.
But what are they? For others greater still
Have passed away, vast oceans have been dried,
Mountains thrown down, the polar star displaced,

The cords that bind the planets rent asunder,
The whole earth deluged with a flood of water,
Even highest angels driven from their stations.
In such a world what relish can there be
For true enjoyment? Deign to rescue us;
Thou only art our refuge, holy lord.

MAITRAYANI UPANISHAD

DAY 178   JUDAISM-
                                                CHRISTIANITY
The Righteous Man

Lord, who shall abide in thy tabernacle?
Who shall dwell in thy holy hill?
He that walketh uprightly, and worketh righteousness, and speak-
eth the truth in his heart.
He that backbiteth not with his tongue, nor doeth evil to his
neighbour, nor taketh up a reproach against his neighbour.
In whose eyes a vile person is contemned; but he honoureth them
that fear the Lord.
He that sweareth to his own hurt, and changeth not.
He that putteth not out his money to usury, nor taketh reward
against the innocent.
He that doeth these things shall never be moved.

PSALM 15

DAY 179   BUDDHISM
Keeping the Sabbath

Once upon a time, when Brahmadatta reigned as king in
Benares, the Buddha-to-be came to life as Sakka, king of the
gods.

At that time a wolf lived on a rock by the bank of the Ganges.
The winter floods came up and surrounded the rock. There he
lay upon the rock, with no food and no way of getting it. The
water rose and rose, and the wolf pondered: "No food here, and

117

no way to get it. Here I lie, with nothing to do. I may as well keep a Sabbath fast."

Sakka, in his meditations, perceived the wolf's weak resolve. Thought he, "I'll plague that wolf"; and taking the shape of a wild goat, he stood near, and let the wolf see him.

"I'll keep the Sabbath another day!" thought the wolf, as he spied him; up he got, and leapt at the creature. But the goat jumped about so that the wolf could not catch him.

When our wolf saw that he could not catch him, he came to a standstill, and went back, thinking to himself as he lay down again, "Well, my Sabbath is not broken after all."

Then Sakka, by his divine power, hovered about in the air; said he, "What have such as you, all unstable, to do with keeping a Sabbath? You didn't know that I was Sakka, and you wanted a meal of goat's flesh!" And thus plaguing and rebuking him, he returned to the world of the gods.

THE JATAKA

DAY 180   STOICISM

True Piety

In piety towards the gods, I would have you know, the chief element is this, to have right opinions about them—as existing and administering the universe well and justly—and to have set yourself to obey them and to submit to everything that happens, and to follow it voluntarily, in the belief that it is being fulfilled by the highest intelligence. For if you act in this way, you will never blame the gods, nor find fault with them for neglecting you. But this result cannot be secured in any other way than by withdrawing your idea of the good and the evil from the things which are not under our control, and placing it in those which are under our control, and in those alone. Because, if you think any of those former things to be good or evil, then, when you fail to get what you want and fall into what you do not want, it is altogether inevitable that you will blame and hate those who are responsible for these results. For this is the nature of every living creature, to flee from and to turn aside from the things that appear harmful, and all that produces them, and to pursue after and to admire the things that are helpful, and all that produces them. Therefore, it is impossible for a man who thinks that he is being hurt to take pleasure in the hurt itself. Hence it follows that even a father is reviled by a son when he does not give his child some share in the things that seem to be good; and this it was which made Polyneices and Eteocles enemies of one another, the thought that the royal power was a good thing. That is why the farmer reviles the gods, and so also the sailor, and the merchant, and those who have lost their wives and their children. For where a man's interest lies, there is also piety. Wherefore, whoever is careful to exercise desire and aversion as he should, is at the same time careful also about piety. But it is always appropriate to make libations, and sacrifices, and to give of the firstfruits after the manner of our fathers, and to do all this with purity, and not in a slovenly or careless fashion, nor, indeed, in a niggardly way, nor yet beyond our means.

EPICTETUS, *Enchiridion*

DAY 181   ISLAM
Presumptuous Man

Recite in the name of thy Lord who created,
Created man from clotted blood.
Recite, for thy Lord is the most generous,
Who taught by the pen,
Taught man what he did not know.
Nay but verily man acts presumptuously
Because he thinks himself independent.
Verily to thy Lord is the return.
Hast thou considered him who restrains
A servant when he prays?
Hast thou considered if he be following the guidance
Or urging to piety?
Hast thou considered if he have counted false, and turned away?
Does he not know that Allah sees?
Nay, but surely, if he do not desist, we shall seize him by the
    forelock,

A lying, sinful forelock.
So let him call his council,
We shall call the imps of Hell.
Nay, obey him not, but do obeisance and draw near.

THE KORAN

DAY 182   CHRISTIANITY

Sacrifice and Love

A little pinch of spice! That is to say: Here a man must be sacrificed, he is needed to impart a particular taste to the rest.

These are the correctives. It is a woeful error if he who is used for applying the corrective becomes impatient and would make the corrective normative for others. That is the temptation to bring everything to confusion.

A little pinch of spice! Humanly speaking, what a painful thing, thus to be sacrificed, to be the little pinch of spice! But on the other hand, God knows well him whom he elects to use in this way, and then he knows also how, in the inward understanding of it, to make it so blessed a thing for him to be sacrificed, that among the thousands of divers voices which express, each in its own way, the same thing, his also will be heard, and perhaps especially his which is truly *de profundis*, proclaiming: God is love. The birds on the branches, the lilies in the field, the deer in the forest, the fishes in the sea, countless hosts of happy men exultantly proclaim: God is love. But beneath all these sopranos, supporting them as it were, as the bass part does, is audible the *de profundis* which issues from the sacrificed one: God is love.

SØREN KIERKEGAARD

DAY 183   CONFUCIANISM

On Being Oneself

The superior man does what is proper to the station in which he is; he does not desire to go beyond this.

In a position of wealth and honor, he does what is proper to a

120

position of wealth and honor. In a poor and low position, he does what is proper to a poor and low position. Situated among barbarous tribes, he does what is proper to a situation among barbarous tribes. In a position of sorrow and difficulty, he does what is proper to a position of sorrow and difficulty. The superior man can find himself in no position in which he is not himself.

In a high situation, he does not treat his inferiors with contempt. In a low situation, he does not court the favor of his superiors. He rectifies himself and seeks for nothing from others, so that he has no dissatisfactions. He does not murmur against heaven or grumble against men.

Thus it is that the superior man is quiet and calm, waiting for the appointments of Heaven, while the mean man walks in dangerous paths, looking for lucky occurrences.

The Master said, "In archery we have something like the way of the superior man. When the archer misses the center of the target, he turns around and seeks for the cause of his failure in himself."

THE DOCTRINE OF THE MEAN

DAY 184   JUDAISM
A Prayer Against Evil

O my God! Guard my tongue from evil and my lips from speaking guile; and to such as curse me let my soul be dumb, yea, let my soul be unto all as the dust. Open my heart to Thy Torah, and let my soul pursue Thy Commandments. And do Thou deliver me from mishap, from the evil impulse, and from an evil woman and all evil which breaks forth to come upon the world. If any design evil against me, speedily make their counsel of none effect, and frustrate their designs. Let the words of my mouth and the meditation of my heart be acceptable before Thee, O Lord, my Rock and Redeemer.

BERAKOTH

The Parable of the Two Sons

And he said unto them . . . But what think ye? A certain man had two sons; and he came to the first, and said, Son, go work to-day in my vineyard. He answered and said, I will not: but afterward he repented, and went. And he came to the second, and said likewise. And he answered and said, I go, sir: and went not. Whether of them twain did the will of his father? They say unto him, The first. Jesus saith unto them, Verily I say unto you, That the publicans and the harlots go into the kingdom of God before you. For John came unto you in the way of righteousness, and ye believed him not: but the publicans and the harlots believed him: and ye, when ye had seen it, repented not afterward, that ye might believe him.

MATTHEW 21:27-32

Types of Men

There are four types of man:

The ordinary one says: "What is mine is mine, and what is yours is yours."

The queer one says: "What is mine is yours, and what is yours is mine."

The saintly one says: "What is mine is yours, and what is yours is yours."

The wicked one says: "What is mine is mine, and what is yours is also mine."

PIRKE ABOTH

The Separation of the Good from the Bad

Who in this world is able to distinguish
The virtuous from the wicked? Both alike

The fruitful earth supports, on both alike
The sun pours down his beams, on both alike
Refreshing breezes blow, and both alike
The waters purify. Not so hereafter—
Then shall the good be severed from the bad.
Then in a region bright with golden luster—
Center of light and immortality—
The righteous after death shall dwell in bliss.
Then a terrific hell awaits the wicked—
Profound abyss of utter misery—
Into the depths of which bad men shall fall
Headlong, and mourn their doom for countless years.

MAHABHARATA

DAY 188   JUDAISM
The Chance To Do Good

One day the Roman Governor, Annius Rufus, asked Rabbi
Akiba: "If your God loves the poor among the Hebrews, why does
he not support them?" "Because God desires to give the rich an
opportunity of doing good," was the Rabbi's reply. "How do you
know that this virtue of charity pleases God," Rufus rejoined,
"since no master can be pleased if a person aids a slave whom he
has seen fit to deprive of food and clothing?" "If for some offense," said Akiba, "the king had deprived his son of food and
drink, and a person had prevented the prince from dying of
hunger, would the king be angry with that person? Certainly not.
Neither will God be displeased with those who dispense charity
to His children, even to the fallen and sinful."

TALMUD

DAY 189   CHRISTIANITY
Fireside Prelates

Msgr. Bolo, protonotary *apostolic,* gives lectures to society
women. "He is the most distinguished among our fireside prelates,"

123

says the *Journal des Débats,* "and one thinks of some rough coun- try priest, poor, living on little, going through mountain paths to visit the sick, and leading to the Lord, amidst icy rocks, sheep that smell of wool grease." Msgr. Bolo belongs to a different school and makes me think of one of our bishops, he too of the fireside brand, who, with his feet up before a good fire and smok- ing a fat cigar after a copious meal, would merrily belch these truthful words: "To think we are the successors of the Apostles!" Bolo is for the royalty of the drawing room, "for perfumes, for good cooking especially," feeling that greediness is an essentially intellectual pleasure and that "the more one is intelligent, the more one ought to be daintily nourished," which somewhat re- moves us from the desert Fathers, upon whom he probably looks as animals. Bolo is a "regenerator." Such preachers are ordinarily brought forth on the eve of catastrophe.

LÉON BLOY

Original Simplicity

Confucius visited Lao Tzu, and spoke of charity and duty to one's neighbor.

Lao Tzu said, "The chaff from winnowing will blind a man's eyes so that he cannot tell the points of the compass. Mosquitoes will keep a man awake all night with their biting. And just in the same way this talk of charity and duty to one's neighbor drives me nearly crazy. Sir! Strive to keep the world to its own original simplicity. And as the wind bloweth where it listeth, so let virtue establish itself. Wherefore such undue energy, as though searching for a fugitive with a big drum?

"The heron is white without a daily bath. The raven is black without daily coloring itself. The original simplicity of black and white is beyond the reach of argument. The vista of fame and reputation is not worthy of enlargement. When the pond dries up and the fish are left upon dry ground, to moisten them with the breath or dampen them with a little spittle is not to be compared with leaving them, in the first instance, in their native rivers and lakes."

On returning from this visit to Lao Tzu, Confucius did not speak for three days. A disciple asked him, "Master, when you saw Lao Tzu, in what direction did you admonish him?"

"I saw a dragon," replied Confucius, "a dragon which by convergence showed a body, by radiation became color, and riding upon the clouds of heaven, nourished the two principles of creation. My mouth was agape: I could not shut it. How then do you think I was going to admonish Lao Tzu?"

CHUANG TZU

DAY 191   CHRISTIANITY

Of Earth and Heaven

God detests plurality;
He thus so draws us in
That all of humankind
Shall in Christ be one.

Three enemies has man:
Self, Beelzebub and World;
Of these three the first one
Is slowest to be felled.

In Heaven one lives well;
No thing is one's own,
What anyone possesses
The Blessed all enjoy.

O mockery! A silkworm
Works till it can fly;
And you stay as you are,
Tethered to the earth.

ANGELUS SILESIUS

The Touching of Hands

Shun-yu K'wan said, "Is it the rule that males and females shall not allow their hands to touch in giving or receiving anything?" Mencius replied, "It is the rule." K'wan asked, "If a man's sister-in-law be drowning, shall he rescue her with his hand?" Mencius said, "He who would not so rescue a drowning woman is a wolf. For males and females not to allow their hands to touch in giving and receiving is the general rule; when a sister-in-law is drowning, to rescue her with the hand is a peculiar exigency."

K'wan said, "The whole empire is drowning. How strange it is that you will not rescue it!"

Mencius answered, "A drowning empire must be rescued with right principles, as a drowning sister-in-law has to be rescued with the hand. Do you wish me to rescue the empire with my hand?"

MENCIUS

Sharp Counsel Concerning Women

Do not be jealous about the wife of your bosom,
And do not teach her an evil lesson, to your own hurt.
Do not give your soul to a woman,
So that she will trample on your strength.
Do not meet a prostitute,
Or you may fall into her snares.
Do not associate with a woman singer,
Or you may be caught by her wiles.
Do not look closely at a girl,
Or you may be entrapped in penalties on her account.

Do not give yourself to prostitutes,
So that you may not lose your inheritance.

126

Do not look around in the streets of the city,
And do not wander about the unfrequented parts of it.
Avert your eyes from a beautiful woman,
And do not look closely at beauty that belongs to someone else.
Many have been led astray by a woman's beauty,
And love is kindled by it like a fire.
Do not ever sit at table with a married woman,
And do not feast and drink with her,
Or your heart may turn away to her,
And you may slip into spiritual ruin.

THE WISDOM OF SIRACH, 9:1-9

DAY 194   JUDAISM
The Law Given in the Wilderness

Why was the Law given in the wilderness? Because if it had
been given in the Promised Land, the tribe on whose territory it
had been given might have said of the other tribes, "I am better
than you." It was given in the wilderness because there all were
equal. Or, again, as in the wilderness there is no sowing or tilling,
so from him who receives the yoke of the Law they remove the
yoke of worldly occupations. . . . Or, again, he who fulfills the
Law makes himself like unto an empty wilderness, and disregards
all other influences.

NUMBERS RABBAH, HUKKAT, XIX, 26

DAY 195   CHRISTIANITY
Tribute to Caesar?

Then went the Pharisees, and took counsel how they might entangle him in his talk. And they sent out unto him their disciples
with the Herodians, saying, Master, we know that thou art true,
and teachest the way of God in truth, neither carest thou for any
man: for thou regardest not the person of men. Tell us therefore,
What thinkest thou? Is it lawful to give tribute unto Caesar, or
not? But Jesus perceived their wickedness, and said, Why tempt

ye me, ye hypocrites? Show me the tribute money. And they brought unto him a penny. And he saith unto them, Whose is this image and superscription? They say unto him, Caesar's. Then saith he unto them, Render therefore unto Caesar the things which are Caesar's; and unto God the things that are God's. When they had heard these words, they marvelled, and left him, and went their way.

MATTHEW 22:15-22

DAY 196   HINDUISM

True Penance

> According to a man's sincerity
> In penitent confession of his crime,
> And detestation of the evil deed,
> Shall he be pardoned and his soul released
> From taint of guilt, like a serpent from its skin.
>
> If he do wrong, 'tis not enough to say
> I will not sin again; release from guilt
> Depends on true contrition, which consists
> In actual abstinence from sinful deeds.

LAW OF MANU

DAY 197   JUDAISM-
                                              CHRISTIANITY

The Psalmist's Shepherd

The Lord is my shepherd; I shall not want.

He maketh me to lie down in green pastures: he leadeth me beside the still waters.

He restoreth my soul: he leadeth me in the paths of righteousness for his name's sake.

Yea, though I walk through the valley of the shadow of death, I will fear no evil: for thou art with me; thy rod and thy staff they comfort me.

Thou preparest a table before me in the presence of mine enemies: thou anointest my head with oil; my cup runneth over.

Surely goodness and mercy shall follow me all the days of my life: and I will dwell in the house of the Lord for ever.

PSALM 23

DAY 198   ANTI-CONFUCIANISM
Condemnation of Offensive War

Now, about a country going to war. If it is in winter it will be too cold; if it is summer it will be too hot. So it should be neither in winter nor in summer. If it is in spring it will take people away from sowing and planting; if it is in autumn it will take people away from reaping and harvesting. Should they be taken away in either of these seasons, innumerable people would die of hunger and cold. And, when the army sets out, the bamboo arrows, the feather flags, the house tents, the armour, the shields, the sword hilts—innumerable quantities of these will break and rot and never come back. The spears, the lances, the swords, the poniards, the chariots, the carts—innumerable quantities of these will break and rot and never come back. Then innumerable horses and oxen will start out fat and come back lean or will not return at all. And innumerable people will die because their food will be cut off and cannot be supplied on account of the great distances of the roads. And innumerable people will be sick and die of the constant danger and the irregularity of eating and drinking and the extremes of hunger and over-eating. Then, the army will be lost in large numbers or entirely; in either case the number will be innumerable. And this means the spirits will lose their worshippers. . . .

Why then does the government deprive the people of their opportunities and benefits to such a great extent? It has been answered: "I covet the fame of the victor and the possessions obtainable through the conquest. So I do it."

. . . But when we consider the victory as such, there is nothing useful about it. When we consider the possessions obtained

129

through it, it does not even make up for the loss. . . . Such an undertaking is not in accordance with the interest of the country.

MOTSE

DAY 199   TAOISM
On Managing Difficulties

Manage the difficult while they are easy;
Manage the great while they are small.
All difficult things in the world start from the easy;
All great things in the world start from the small.
The tree that fills a man's arms arises from a tender shoot;
The nine-storied tower is raised from a heap of earth;
A thousand miles' journey begins from the spot under one's feet.
Therefore the sage never attempts great things, and thus he can
  achieve what is great.
He who makes easy promises will seldom keep his word;
He who regards many things easy will find many difficulties.
Therefore the sage regards things difficult, and consequently
  never has difficulties.

TAO-TE-KING

DAY 200   ISLAM
Rewards and Punishments

In the Name of God, the Merciful, the Compassionate
By the night enshrouding
and the day in splendour
and That which created the male and the female,
surely your striving is to diverse ends.

As for him who gives and is godfearing
and confirms the reward most fair,
We shall surely ease him to the Easing.
But as for him who is a miser, and self-sufficient,
and cries lies to the reward most fair,

130

We shall surely ease him to the Hardship;
his wealth shall not avail him when he perishes.

Surely upon Us rests the guidance,
and to Us belong the Last and the First.

Now I have warned you of a Fire that flames,
whereat none but the most wretched shall be roasted,
even he who cried lies, and turned away;
and from which the most godfearing shall be removed,
even he who gives his wealth to purify himself
and confers no favour on any man for recompense,
only seeking the Face of his Lord the Most High;
and he shall surely be satisfied.

THE KORAN

HINDUISM

True Wealth

Before infirmities creep over your flesh;
Before decay impairs your strength and mars
The beauty of your limbs; before the Ender,
Whose charioteer is sickness, hastes toward you,
Breaks up your fragile frame and ends your life,
Lay up the only treasure: do good deeds;
Practice sobriety and self-control;
Amass that wealth which thieves cannot rob you of,
Nor tyrants seize, which follows you at death,
Which never wastes away, nor is corrupted.

MAHABHARATA

DAY 202   CHRISTIANITY

The Ten Virgins

Then shall the kingdom of heaven be likened unto ten virgins,
which took their lamps, and went forth to meet the bridegroom.
And five of them were wise, and five were foolish. They that

were foolish took their lamps, and took no oil with them. But the wise took oil in their vessels with their lamps. While the bridegroom tarried, they all slumbered and slept. And at midnight there was a cry made, Behold, the bridegroom cometh; go ye out to meet him. Then all those virgins arose, and trimmed their lamps. And the foolish said unto the wise, Give us of your oil; for our lamps are gone out. But the wise answered, saying, Not so; lest there be not enough for us and you: but go ye rather to them that sell, and buy for yourselves. And while they went to buy, the bridegroom came; and they that were ready went in with him to the marriage: and the door was shut. Afterward came also the other virgins, saying, Lord, Lord, open to us. But he answered and said, Verily I say unto you, I know you not. Watch therefore, for ye know neither the day nor the hour wherein the Son of man cometh.

MATTHEW 25:1-13

DAY 203   TAOISM
The Pursuit of Knowledge

Without going out of the door
One can know the whole world;
Without peeping out of the window
One can see the Tao of heaven.
The further one travels
The less one knows.
Therefore the sage knows everything without traveling;
He names everything without seeing it;
He accomplishes everything without doing it.

TAO-TE-KING

DAY 204   CHRISTIANITY
Forgiving a Thief

One Nicias, a philosopher, had his shoes stolen from him. May they, said he, fit his feet that took them away. A wish at the first view very harmless, but there was that in it which

132

poisoned his charity into a malicious revenge. For he himself had hurled or crooked feet, so that in effect he wished the thief to be lame.

Whosoever hath plundered me of my books and papers, I freely forgive him; and desire he may fully understand and make good use thereof, wishing him more joy of them than he hath right to them. Nor is there any snake under my herbs, nor have I (as Nicias) any reservation, or latent sense to myself, but from my heart do desire, that to all purposes and intents my books may be beneficial unto him. Only requesting him, that one passage in his (lately my) Bible (namely, Eph. IV. 28) may be taken into his serious consideration.

THOMAS FULLER

DAY 205   JUDAISM
The Whole Law

Once a Gentile came to Shamai and said, "Proselytize me, but on condition that thou teach me the whole law, even the whole of it, while I stand upon one leg." Shamai drove him off with the builder's rod which he held in his hand. When he came to Hillel with the same challenge, Hillel converted him by answering him on the spot, "That which is hateful to thyself, do not do to thy neighbor. This is the whole law, and the rest is commentary."

SHABBATH

DAY 206   CHRISTIANITY
The Divine Image

Jesus said: "Wouldest thou love one who never died
For thee, or ever die for one who had not died for thee?
And if God dieth not for Man, and giveth not Himself
Eternally for Man, Man could not exist; for Man is Love,
As God is Love: every kindness to another is a little Death
In the Divine Image; nor can Man exist but by Brotherhood."

WILLIAM BLAKE, *Jerusalem*

133

Adoration

To thee be sung a thousand hymns of praise
By every creature and from every quarter,
Before, above, behind. Hail! Hail! thou All!
Again and yet again I worship thee.
Have mercy, I implore thee, and forgive,
That I, in ignorance of this thy glory,
Presumed to call thee Friend; and pardon too
Whate'er I have too negligently uttered,
Addressing thee in too familiar tones.
Unrivaled God of gods, I fall before thee
Prostrate in adoration, thou the Father
Of all that lives and lives not; have compassion,
Bear with me, as a father with a son,
Or as a lover with a cherished one.
Now that I see thee as thou really art,
I thrill with terror! Mercy! Lord of lords,
Once more display to me thy human form,
Thou habitation of the universe.

BHAGAVAD-GITA

Duty to Neighbor

Withhold not good from them to whom it is due, when it is
in the power of thine hand to do it. Say not unto thy neighbour,
Go, and come again, and tomorrow I will give; when thou hast
it by thee. Devise not evil against thy neighbour, seeing he
dwelleth securely by thee. Strive not with a man without cause,
if he have done thee no harm. Envy thou not the oppressor, and
choose none of his ways. For the froward is abomination to the
Lord: but his secret is with the righteous. The curse of the Lord

is in the house of the wicked: but he blesseth the habitation of the just. Surely he scorneth the scorners: but he giveth grace unto the lowly. The wise shall inherit glory: but shame shall be the promotion of fools.

PROVERBS 3:27-35

DAY 209   ANTI-CONFUCIANISM
Righteousness in Government

Those gentlemen of the world who desire to do righteousness have only to obey the will of Heaven. To obey the will of Heaven is to be universal and to oppose the will of Heaven is to be partial (in love). According to the doctrine of universality, righteousness is the standard; in the doctrine of partiality, force is the basis of government. What is it like to have righteousness as the basis of government? The great will not attack the small, the strong will not plunder the weak, the many will not oppress the few, the clever will not deceive the ignorant, the honored will not disdain the humble, the rich will not mock the poor, and the young will not rob the old, And the states in the empire will not ruin each other with water, fire, poison, and weapons.

MOTSE

DAY 210   CHRISTIANITY
The Last Judgment

When the Son of man shall come in his glory, and all the holy angels with him, then shall he sit upon the throne of his glory: And before him shall be gathered all nations; and he shall separate them one from another, as a shepherd divideth his sheep from the goats: And he shall set the sheep on his right hand, but the goats on the left. Then shall the King say unto them on his right hand, Come, ye blessed of my Father, inherit the kingdom prepared for you from the foundation of the world: For I was an hungred, and ye gave me meat: I was thirsty, and ye gave me drink: I was a stranger, and ye took me in: Naked, and ye clothed me: I was sick, and ye visited me: I was in prison, and

135

ye came unto me. . . . Then shall he say also unto them on the left hand, Depart from me, ye cursed, into everlasting fire, prepared for the devil and his angels: For I was an hungred, and ye gave me no meat: I was thirsty, and ye gave me no drink: I was a stranger, and ye took me not in: naked, and ye clothed me not: sick, and in prison, and ye visited me not. Then shall they also answer him, saying, Lord, when saw we thee an hungred, or athirst, or a stranger, or naked, or sick, or in prison, and did not minister unto thee? Then shall he answer them, saying, Verily I say unto you, Inasmuch as ye did it not to one of the least of these, ye did it not to me. And these shall go away into everlasting punishment: but the righteous into life eternal.

MATTHEW 25:31-36, 41-46

DAY 2 I I   TAOISM
Knowing Oneself

He who knows others is learned;
    He who knows himself is wise.
He who conquers others has power of muscles;
    He who conquers himself is strong.
He who is contented is rich.
    He who is determined has strength of will.
He who does not lose his center endures,
He who dies yet (his power) remains has long life.

TAO-TE-KING

DAY 2 I 2   CHRISTIANITY
On Weak and Imperfect Conversions

People who have lived far from God are apt to think themselves very near Him as soon as they make some steps toward Him.

Thus polished and enlightened men make the same mistake as the peasant does, who thinks he has been at court because he has seen the king. They quit their most heinous vices and adopt

136

a rather less criminal life, but still effeminate, worldly, and vain; they judge of themselves, not by the Gospel, which is the only rule they ought to follow, but by a comparison between their present life and the one they formerly led.

This is enough, they think, to canonize them; and they remain in a profound tranquility as to what is yet to be done for their salvation. Such a state is perhaps more to be apprehended than one of open sin, for this might awaken conscience, and faith might revive, and they might make a great effort; while the other state only serves to stifle salutary remorse, and establish a false peace in the heart that renders the evil irremediable.

These Christians are low-minded and cowardly; they would possess heaven at a low price; they do not think of what it has cost those who have obtained it; they do not consider what is due to God.

Such men are far from being converted. If the Gospel had been confided to them, it would not have been what it is now; we should have had something far more pleasing to our self-love. But the Gospel is immutable, and it is by that we must be judged. Let us follow this sure guide, and fear nothing so much as to be flattered and betrayed.

FRANÇOIS DE FÉNELON

DAY 213   JUDAISM
Kindness to Those in Need

He who does an act of kindness to those who really need it, will have a greater reward than that of Abraham, who showed hospitality to angels. Abraham stood under a tree and waited on the three strangers while they ate and drank. And what reward had his descendants? The manna came down to them, and the springs of water rose up for them; quails came around them for their food, and the cloud of the Divine Glory stood to watch over them. But Abraham's guests were angels, who needed nothing: how much greater, then, will be the reward of those whose kindness is done to the poor, who need all things?

BARMIDBAR RABBAH

CONFUCIANISM
Semblance versus Reality

I hate a semblance which is not the reality. I hate the darnel,
lest it be confounded with the corn. I hate glib-tonguedness, lest
it be confounded with righteousness. I hate sharpness of tongue,
lest it be confounded with sincerity. I hate the music of Ch'ing,
lest it be confounded with the true music. I hate the reddish blue,
lest it be confounded with vermilion. I hate your good, careful
men of the villages, lest they be confounded with the truly virtuous.

CONFUCIUS

DAY 215 ISLAM
The Soul of Goodness in Things Evil

Fools take false coins because they are like the true.
If in the world no genuine minted coin
Were current, how would forgers pass the false?
Falsehood were nothing unless truth were there,
To make it specious. 'Tis the love of right
Lures men to wrong. Let poison but be mixed
With sugar, they will cram it into their mouths.
Oh, cry not that all creeds are vain! Some scent
Of truth they have, else they would not beguile.
Say not, "How utterly fantastical!"
No fancy in the world is all untrue.
Amidst the crowd of dervishes hides one,
One true fakir. Search well and thou wilt find!

JALALU'L-DIN RUMI

DAY 216 ZOROASTRIANISM
Essential Differences

He that does not restore a loan to the man who lent it steals
the thing and robs the man. This he doeth every day, every night,

as long as he keep in his house his neighbor's property, as though it were his own. . . .

Verily I say it unto thee, O Spitama Zarathustra! the man who has a wife is far above him who lives in continence; he who keeps a house is far above him who has none; he who has children is far above the childless man; he who has riches is far above him who has none.

And of two men, he who fills himself with meat receives in him Good Thought much better than he who does not do so; the latter is all but dead; the former is above him by the worth of . . . a man.

VENDIDAD

DAY 217   CHRISTIANITY
The First Two Commandments

And one of the scribes came, and having heard them reasoning together, and perceiving that he had answered them well, asked him, Which is the first commandment of all? And Jesus answered him, The first of all the commandments is, Hear, O Israel; The Lord our God is one Lord: and thou shalt love the Lord thy God with all thy heart, and with all thy soul, and with all thy mind, and with all thy strength: this is the first commandment. And the second is like, namely this, Thou shalt love thy neighbour as thyself. There is none other commandment greater than these. And the scribe said unto him, Well, Master, thou hast said the truth: for there is one God; and there is none other but he: And to love him with all the heart, and with all the understanding, and with all the soul, and with all the strength, and to love his neighbour as himself, is more than all whole burnt offerings and sacrifices. And when Jesus saw that he answered discreetly, he said unto him, Thou art not far from the kingdom of God. And no man after that durst ask him any question.

MARK 12:28-34

Subjectivity

Once upon a time, during the reign of Brahmadatta, king of Benares, the Bodhisattva became a tree sprite on the bank of the Ganges. At the point where the Ganges and Jumna meet, two fish met together, one from the Ganges and one from the Jumna. "I am beautiful!" said one, "and so are you!" and then they fell to quarreling about their beauty. Not far from the Ganges they saw a tortoise lying on the bank. "That fellow shall decide whether or not we are beautiful!" they said, and they went up to him. "Which of us is beautiful, friend tortoise," they asked, "the Ganges fish or the Jumna fish?" The tortoise answered, "The Ganges fish is beautiful, and the Jumna fish is beautiful, but I am more beautiful than you both." And to explain it, he uttered the first verse:

"Fine are the fish of Jumna stream, the Ganges fish are fine,
But a four-footed creature, with a tapering neck like mine,
Round like a spreading banyan tree, must all of them outshine."

When the fish heard this, they cried, "Ah, you rascally tortoise! You won't answer our question, but you answer another one!" and they repeated the second verse:

"We ask him this, he answers that: indeed a strange reply!
By his own tongue his praise is sung: I like it not, not I!"

THE JATAKA

A Gulf of Empty Words

I have just undergone a terrible sermon against Materialism or Naturalism as opposed to supernatural Revelation. All the philosophic platitudes of the seminary paraded before the Blessed Sacrament, motionless in the tabernacle. I, alas! had come to the church like "a beggar full of prayers." That gulf of empty words swallowed them up, and my soul slipped into the uneasy slumber that dull prattle induces. In the very face of the Enemy, such, then, is the concern of preachers, for how many long years brought up and carefully tended in scorn of the warnings of La Salette—on the eve of a frightful day of reckoning!

What systematic deformation of the faith, or what lack of it, must we assume to account for such ministers, and so great a number of them, having come to the point—where they no longer know that man's stock in trade is Faith and Obedience, and that consequently he needs Apostles and not lecturers, Witnesses and not demonstrators. The day has gone for proving that God exists. The hour strikes when one must give one's life for Jesus Christ.

LÉON BLOY

DAY 220   JUDAISM

The Presence of the Lord

Commenting on Exodus 17:7—"Is the Lord among us or not?" —our sages say that for this want of faith the Israelites were brought in contact with their enemy Amelek. This matter may be likened to the parable of a child who is riding on his father's shoulders, and on meeting a friend of his father's, calls out: "Have you seen my father anywhere?" Then his father sayeth unto him: "Thou art riding on my shoulders, and thou asketh questions about me. I will put thee down for a moment in the presence of the enemy, so as to teach thee what my absence would mean."

SHEMOTH RABBATH

DAY 221   TAOISM

The Four Eternal Models

Before the Heaven and Earth existed
There was something nebulous:
    Silent, isolated,
    Standing alone, changing not,

Eternally revolving without fail,
Worthy to be the Mother of All Things.
I do not know its name
    And address it as Tao.
If forced to give it a name, I shall call it "Great."
Being great implies reaching out in space,
Reaching out in space implies far-reaching,
Far-reaching implies reversion to the original point.

Therefore: Tao is Great,
            The Heaven is great,
            The Earth is great,
            The King is also great.
These are the Great Four in the universe,
And the King is one of them.

Man models himself after the Earth;
The Earth models itself after Heaven;
The Heaven models itself after Tao;
Tao models itself after Nature.

                                    TAO-TE-KING

DAY 222   ISLAM

The Most High

In the Name of God, the Merciful, the Compassionate

Magnify the Name of thy Lord the Most High
        who created and shaped,
        who determined and guided,
        who brought forth the pasturage
        then made it a blackening wrack.

We shall make thee recite, to forget not
        save what God wills;
    surely He knows what is spoken aloud
            and what is hidden.
    We shall ease thee unto the Easing.

Therefore remind, if the Reminder profits,
and he who fears shall remember,
but the most wretched shall flout it,
even he who shall roast in the Great Fire,
then he shall neither die therein, nor live.

Prosperous is he who has cleansed himself,
and mentions the Name of his Lord, and prays.

Nay, but you prefer the present life;
and the world to come is better, and more enduring.

Surely this is in the ancient scrolls,
the scrolls of Abraham and Moses.

THE KORAN

DAY 223   JUDAISM-
                              CHRISTIANITY
God a Refuge and Help

God is our refuge and strength, a very present help in trouble.

Therefore will not we fear, though the earth be removed, and though the mountains be carried into the midst of the sea;

Though the waters thereof roar and be troubled, though the mountains shake with the swelling thereof.

There is a river, the streams whereof shall make glad the city of God, the holy place of the tabernacles of the Most High.

God is in the midst of her; she shall not be moved: God shall help her, and that right early.

The heathen raged, the kingdoms were moved: he uttered his voice, the earth melted.

The Lord of hosts is with us; the God of Jacob is our refuge.

Come, behold the works of the Lord, what desolations he hath made in the earth.

He maketh wars to cease unto the end of the earth; he breaketh the bow, and cutteth the spear in sunder; he burneth the chariot in the fire.

Be still, and know that I am God: I will be exalted among the heathen, I will be exalted in the earth.

The Lord of hosts is with us; the God of Jacob is our refuge.

PSALM 46

DAY 224   ZOROASTRIANISM

Purification

When the sun rises up, purification comes upon the earth made by Ahura, purification unto the flowing waters, unto the waters of the wells, unto the water of the seas, unto the water that is standing. Purification comes unto the righteous creation, which is of the holy spirits. If indeed the sun were not to rise, then the demons would kill all things that are in the seven regions. He who offers up a sacrifice unto the undying, shining, swift-horsed Sun—to withstand darkness, to withstand the Daevas born of darkness, to withstand the robbers and bandits . . . to withstand death that creeps in unseen—offers it up to Ahura Mazda . . . offers it up to his own soul. . . . I bless the sacrifice and the invocation, and the strength and vigor of the undying, shining, swift-horsed Sun.

YASHT

DAY 225   JUDAISM-
                                           CHRISTIANITY

Four Similes

A word fitly spoken
Is like apples of gold in network of silver.
As an earring of gold, and an ornament of fine gold,
So is a wise reprover upon an obedient ear.
As the cold of snow in the time of harvest,
So is a faithful messenger to them that send him:
For he refresheth the soul of his masters.
As clouds and wind without rain,
So is he that boasteth himself of his gifts falsely.

PROVERBS 25:11-14

144

DAY 226   JUDAISM
Righteousness and Justice

Do not sneer at justice, for it is one of the three feet of the
world, for the sages taught that the world stands on three things:
justice, truth and peace. Therefore reflect that if you pervert
justice, you shake the world, because justice is one of its three
feet. . . . It is written, "To do justice and righteousness is
better than sacrifice" (Proverbs 21:3). For sacrifices could be
brought only when the Temple existed, but justice and righteousness can be applied both then and after. Sacrifices atone only for
involuntary sins, but justice and righteousness atone both for
voluntary and involuntary sins; sacrifices are brought only by
men, but justice and righteousness are used also by the world
above [i.e., in heaven, among the angels]. Sacrifices can occur
only in this world, but righteousness and justice are for this
world and for the world to come.

SIMEON BEN GABRIEL

DAY 227   BUDDHISM
Where Is the Puppet's Maker?

By whom was wrought this puppet?
Where is the puppet's maker?
And where does the puppet arise?
Where is the puppet stopped?

Not made by the self is this puppet,
Nor is this misfortune made by others.
Conditioned by cause it comes to be,
By breaking of cause is it stopped.

. . . .

By whom was wrought this being?
Where is the being's maker?
Where does the being arise?
Where is the being stopped?

Why do you harp on "being"?
It is a false view for you.
A mere heap of samkharas, this—
Here no "being" is got at.

For as when the parts are rightly set
We utter the word "chariot"
So when there are the khandhas—
By convention, "there is a being," we say.

For it is simply suffering that comes to be,
Suffering that perishes and wanes,
Not other than suffering comes to be,
Naught else than suffering is stopped.

SAMYUTTA NIKAYA

DAY 228   CHRISTIANITY

Attaining Spiritual Perfection

You see that the mountain of Christian perfection is exceedingly high. O my God! you say, how shall I be able to ascend it? Courage, Philothea! When the young bees begin to take shape, we call them nymphs. As yet they are unable to fly to the flowers, the mountains, or the neighboring hills in order to gather honey. Little by little, by continuing to feed on the honey which the old ones have prepared, the little nymphs take on wings and acquire sufficient strength to fly and seek their food all over the country. It is true we are as yet but little bees in devotion. Consequently, we are unable to fly up high in accordance with our plan, which is nothing less than to reach the peak of Christian perfection. Yet, as our desires and resolutions begin to assume a form, and as our wings begin to grow, we hope that we shall one day become spiritual bees and be able to fly. In the meantime let us feed upon the honey of the many good instructions that devout persons of ancient days have left us. Let us pray to God to give us "wings like a dove," that we may not only be enabled to fly upward during the time of this present life, but also to rest ourselves in the eternity that is to come.

ST. FRANCIS DE SALES

Men of True Breeding

A high official of Sung asked about "men of honor," and the Master said, "A man of honor has no self-pity and no fears." The official replied, "Is that all it means?" The Master said, "When he examines his heart and finds no taint, what cause has he for self-pity or for fear? Men of true breeding are in harmony with people, although they do not agree with them; but men of no breeding agree with people, and yet are not in harmony with them.

"A man of true breeding is easy to serve but hard to please: for if you try to please him by any other means than the Way, he is not pleased. When he sets men their tasks, it is as appropriate tools for appropriate jobs. A man of no breeding is hard to serve but easy to please: for you can please him by other means than the Way. But when it is a matter of setting men tasks, he expects them to be ready for anything.

"Men of true breeding have dignity but are not arrogant. Men of no breeding are arrogant but have no dignity.

"Men of true breeding are ashamed for their words to go beyond their deeds."

Tzu Lu asked about men of true breeding, and the Master said, "They bring their personality into flower with a view to reverent action." Tzu Lu asked if this were all, and the Master said, "They bring their personality into flower in order that they may bring peace to other men." Tzu Lu again asked whether this was all, and the Master said, "They bring their personality into flower in order that they may bring peace to every family and clan. If they do that, could even Yao or Shun find fault with them?"

ANALECTS

Mighty Lord of All

I see thee, mighty Lord of all, revealed
In forms of infinite diversity.

I see thee like a mass of purest light,
Flashing thy luster everywhere around.
I see thee crowned with splendor like the sun,
Pervading earth and sky, immeasurable,
Boundless, without beginning, middle, end,
Preserver of imperishable law,
The everlasting Man; the triple world
Is awe-struck at this vision of thy form,
Stupendous, indescribable in glory.
Have mercy, God of gods; the universe
Is fitly dazzled by thy majesty,
Fitly to thee alone devotes its homage.
At thy approach the evil demons flee,
Scattered in terror to the winds of heaven.
The multitude of holy saints adore thee—
Thee, first Creator, lord of all the gods,
The ancient One, supreme Receptacle
Of all that is and is not, knowing all,
And to be known by all. Immensely vast,
Thou comprehendest all, thou art the All.

BHAGAVAD-GITA

DAY 231   JUDAISM-
                                              CHRISTIANITY
Praise and Worship God

O come, let us sing unto the Lord: let us make a joyful noise to the rock of our salvation.

Let us come before his presence with thanksgiving, and make a joyful noise unto him with psalms.

For the Lord is a great God, and a great King above all gods.

In his hand are the deep places of the earth: the strength of the hills is his also.

The sea is his, and he made it: and his hands formed the dry land.

O come, let us worship and bow down: let us kneel before the Lord our maker.

148

For he is our God; and we are the people of his pasture, and the sheep of his hand. To day if ye will hear his voice,

Harden not your heart, as in the provocation, and as in the day of temptation in the wilderness:

When your fathers tempted me, proved me, and saw my work.

Forty years long was I grieved with this generation, and said, It is a people that do err in their heart, and they have not known my ways:

Unto whom I sware in my wrath, that they should not enter into my rest.

PSALM 95

DAY 232   TAOISM

The Way of Heaven

True words are not fine-sounding;
    Fine-sounding words are not true.
A good man does not argue;
    He who argues is not a good man.
The wise one does not know many things;
    He who knows many things is not wise.

The Sage does not accumulate (for himself):
    He lives for other people,
    And grows richer himself;
    He gives to other people,
    And has greater abundance.

The Tao of Heaven
    Blesses, but does not harm.
The Way of the Sage
    Accomplishes, but does not contend.

TAO-TE-KING

The Good Samaritan

And, behold, a certain lawyer stood up, and tempted him, saying, Master, what shall I do to inherit eternal life?

He said unto him, What is written in the law? how readest thou?

And he answering said, Thou shalt love the Lord thy God with all thy heart, and with all thy soul, and with all thy strength, and with all thy mind; and thy neighbour as thyself.

And he said unto him, Thou hast answered right: this do, and thou shalt live.

But he, willing to justify himself, said unto Jesus, And who is my neighbour?

And Jesus answering said, A certain man went down from Jerusalem to Jericho, and fell among thieves, which stripped him of his raiment, and wounded him, and departed, leaving him half dead. And by chance there came down a certain priest that way; and when he saw him, he passed by on the other side. And likewise a Levite, when he was at the place, came and looked on him, and passed by on the other side. But a certain Samaritan, as he journeyed, came where he was, and when he saw him, he had compassion on him, and went to him, and bound up his wounds, pouring in oil and wine, and set him on his own beast, and brought him to an inn, and took care of him. And on the morrow when he departed, he took out two pence, and gave them to the host, and said unto him, Take care of him: and whatsoever thou spendest more, when I come again, I will repay thee.

Which now of these three, thinkest thou, was neighbour unto him that fell among the thieves?

And he said, He that showed mercy on him. Then said Jesus unto him, Go, and do thou likewise.

LUKE 10:25-37

The Parable of the Saw

"Brethren, there are these five ways of speech which other men may use to you: speech seasonable or unseasonable, speech true or false, speech gentle or bitter, speech conducive to profit or loss, speech kindly or resentful.

"When men speak evil of you, thus must you train yourselves: 'Our heart shall be unwavering, no evil word will we send forth, but compassionate of others' welfare will we abide, of kindly heart without resentment, and that man who thus speaks will we suffuse with thoughts accompanied by love, and so abide. And, making that our standpoint, we will suffuse the whole world with loving thoughts, far-reaching, wide-spreading, boundless, free from hate, free from ill-will, and so abide.' Thus, brethren must you train yourselves.

"Moreover, brethren, though highwaymen should with a two-handed saw carve you in pieces limb by limb, yet if the mind of any one of you should be offended at this, such a one is no follower of my gospel. But thus (as I have shown you) must you train yourselves. . . .

"And this parable of the Saw which I have taught you, bear it in mind again and yet again. Do you not see, brethren, that there is no syllable thereof, either small or great, but you must agree thereto?"

"Surely, Lord."

"Wherefore, brethren, bear in mind this parable of the Saw that I have now taught you, for it shall be to your profit and welfare for many a long day."

MAJJHIMA NIKAYA

Life Is Risk

When you put a cargo on board a ship, you make that venture on trust,

For you know not whether you will be drowned or come safe to land.

If you say, "I will not embark till I am certain of my fate," then you will do no trade: the secret of these two destinies is never disclosed.

The faint-hearted merchant neither gains nor loses; nay he loses: one must take fire in order to get light.

Since all affairs turn upon hope, surely Faith is the best object of hope, for thereby you win salvation.

JALALU'L-DIN RUMI

DAY 236

JUDAISM-
CHRISTIANITY

Praise the Lord Who Reigneth

O sing unto the Lord a new song: sing unto the Lord, all the earth.

Sing unto the Lord, bless his name; shew forth his salvation from day to day.

Declare his glory among the heathen, his wonders among all people.

For the Lord is great, and greatly to be praised: he is to be feared above all gods.

For all the gods of the nations are idols: but the Lord made the heavens.

Honour and majesty are before him: strength and beauty are in his sanctuary.

Give unto the Lord, O ye kindreds of the people, give unto the Lord glory and strength.

Give unto the Lord the glory due unto his name: bring an offering, and come into his courts.

O worship the Lord in the beauty of holiness: fear before him, all the earth.

Say among the heathen that the Lord reigneth: the world also shall be established that it shall not be moved: he shall judge the people righteously.

Let the heavens rejoice, and let the earth be glad; let the sea roar, and the fullness thereof.

152

Let the field be joyful, and all that is therein: then shall all the trees of the wood rejoice

Before the Lord: for he cometh, for he cometh to judge the earth: he shall judge the world with righteousness, and the people with his truth.

PSALM 96

DAY 237   CONFUCIANISM

The Central Harmony

What is God-given is what we call human nature. To fulfil the law of our human nature is what we call the moral law. The cultivation of the moral law is what we call culture.

The moral law is a law from whose operation we cannot for one instant in our existence escape. A law from which we may escape is not the moral law. Wherefore it is that the moral man (or the superior man) watches diligently over what his eyes cannot see and is in fear and awe of what his ears cannot hear.

There is nothing more evident than that which cannot be seen by the eyes and nothing more palpable than that which cannot be perceived by the senses. Wherefore the moral man watches diligently over his secret thoughts.

When the passions, such as joy, anger, grief, and pleasure, have not awakened, that is our *central* self, or moral being (*chung*). When these passions awaken and each and all attain due measure and degree, that is *harmony*, or the moral order (*ho*). Our central self or moral being is the great basis of existence, and *harmony* or moral order is the universal law in the world.

When our true central self and harmony are realized, the universe then becomes a cosmos and all things attain their full growth and development.

CONFUCIUS

153

Divine Solitude

Birds have their nests in trees, to which they may retire when they have need, and the deer have bushes and thickets in which they conceal themselves and enjoy the cool shade in the heat of summer. So should our hearts, Philothea, choose some place every day, either on Mount Calvary or in the wounds of our Lord or in some other place near Him, as a retreat to which they may occasionally retire to refresh and recreate themselves amidst their exterior occupations, and there, as in a stronghold, defend themselves against temptations. Blessed is the soul that can say with truth to the Lord: "Thou art my place of strength and my refuge, my defense from storms, and my shadow from the heat."

Remember then, Philothea, to retire occasionally into the solitude of your heart while you are outwardly engaged in business or association with others. This mental solitude cannot be prevented by the multitude of those who surround you. As they are not about your heart, but only about your body, your heart may remain in the presence of God alone. This was the exercise which King David practiced amidst his various occupations. To this he himself testifies a thousand times in his Psalms, as when he says: "O Lord, I am always with Thee." "I set the Lord always before me in my sight." "To Thee I have lifted up my eyes, O my God, who dwellest in heaven." "My eyes are ever toward the Lord." Indeed our occupations are seldom so serious as to prevent us from withdrawing our heart occasionally from them, in order to retire into this divine solitude.

ST. FRANCIS DE SALES

Ways of Survival

To yield is to be preserved whole.
To be bent is to become straight.
To be hollow is to be filled.

To be tattered is to be renewed.
To be in want is to possess.
To have plenty is to be confused.

Therefore the Sage embraces the One,
And becomes the model of the world.
He does not reveal himself,
    And is therefore luminous.
He does not justify himself,
    And is therefore far-famed.
He does not boast of himself,
    And therefore people give him credit.
He does not pride himself,
    And is therefore the chief among men.

It is because he does not contend
That no one in the world can contend against him.

Is it not indeed true, as the ancients say,
    "To yield is to be preserved whole"?
Thus he is preserved and the world does him homage.

TAO-TE-KING

DAY 240   CHRISTIANITY
On the Anxieties of Life

And he said unto his disciples, Therefore I say unto you, Take
no thought for your life, what ye shall eat; neither for the body,
what ye shall put on. The life is more than meat, and the body
is more than raiment. Consider the ravens: for they neither sow
nor reap; which neither have storehouse nor barn; and God
feedeth them: how much more are ye better than the fowls? And
which of you with taking thought can add to his stature one
cubit? If ye then be not able to do that thing which is least, why
take ye thought for the rest? Consider the lilies how they grow:
they toil not, they spin not; and yet I say unto you, that Solomon
in all his glory was not arrayed like one of these. If then God
so clothe the grass, which is to-day in the field, and to-morrow is

155

cast into the oven; how much more will he clothe you, O ye of little faith? And seek not ye what ye shall eat, or what ye shall drink, neither be ye of doubtful mind. For all these things do the nations of the world seek after: and your Father knoweth that ye have need of these things.

But rather seek ye the Kingdom of God; and all these things shall be added unto you.

LUKE 12:22-31

Let Us Not Forget Thy Name!

Were a mansion of pearls erected and inlaid with gems for me;
Perfumed with musk, saffron, fragrant aloes and sandal to confer delight;
May it not be that on beholding these things I may forget Thee, O God, and not remember Thy Name!
My soul burneth without Thee.
I have ascertained from my Guru that there is no other shelter than in God.
Were the earth to be studded with diamonds and rubies, and my couch to be similarly adorned;
Were fascinating damsels whose faces were decked with jewels to shed lustre and enhance the pleasure of the scene;
May it not be that on beholding them I may forget Thee and not remember Thy Name!
Were I to become a Sidh and work miracles; could I command the wealth of the universe to come to me;
Could I disappear and appear at pleasure, and were the world to honour me;
May it not be that on beholding these things I may forget Thee and not remember Thy Name!
Were I to become a monarch on my throne and raise an army;
Were dominion and regal revenue mine—O Nanak, they would be all worthless—
May it not be that on beholding these things I may forget Thee and not remember Thy Name!

NANAK

The Majesty of God

What god shall we adore with sacrifice?
Him let us praise, the golden child that rose
In the beginning, who was born the lord—
The one sole lord of all that is—who made
The earth, and formed the sky, who giveth life,
Who giveth strength, whose bidding gods revere,
Whose hiding-place is immortality,
Whose shadow, death; who by his might is king
Of all the breathing, sleeping, waking world—
Who governs men and beasts, whose majesty
These snowy hills, this ocean with its rivers
Declare; of whom these spreading regions form
The arms; by whom the firmament is strong,
Earth firmly planted, and the highest heavens
Supported, and the clouds that fill the air
Distributed and measured out; to whom
Both earth and heaven, established by his will,
Look up with trembling mind; in whom revealed
The rising sun shines forth above the world.
Wherever let loose in space, the mighty waters
Have gone, depositing a fruitful seed
And generating fire, there he arose
Who is the breath and life of all the gods,
Whose mighty glance looks around the vast expanse
Of watery vapour—source of energy,
Cause of the sacrifice—the only God
Above the gods. May he not injure us!
He the Creator of the earth—the righteous
Creator of the sky, Creator too
Of oceans bright, and far-extending waters.

RIGVEDA

157

A Prayer for the Morning

O my God, the soul which thou gavest me is pure; thou didst create it, thou didst form it, thou didst breathe it into me; thou preservest it within me; and thou wilt take it away from me, but wilt restore it unto me hereafter. So long as the soul is within me, I will give thanks unto thee, O Lord my God and God of my fathers, Sovereign of all worlds, Lord of all souls! Blessed art thou, O Lord, who restorest souls into the dead.

BERAKOTH

The Golden Rule

Chung Kung asked about true manhood, and Confucius replied, "When the true man appears abroad, he feels as if he were receiving distinguished people, and when ruling over the people, he feels as if he were worshiping God. What he does not want done unto himself, he does not do unto others. And so both in the state and in the home, people are satisfied."

Tsekung said, "What I do not want others to do unto me, I do not want to do unto them." Confucius said, "Ah Sze, you cannot do it."

Confucius said, "Ah Ts'an, there is a central principle that runs through all my teachings." "Yes," said Tsengtse. When Confucius left, the disciples asked Tsengtse what he meant, and Tsengtse replied, "It is just the principle of reciprocity (or *shu*)."

Tsekung asked, "Is there one single word that can serve as a principle of conduct for life?" Confucius replied, "Perhaps the word 'reciprocity' (*shu*) will do. Do not do unto others what you do not want others to do unto you."

ANALECTS

Praise for God's Great Mercies

Bless the Lord, O my soul: and all that is within me, bless his holy name.

Bless the Lord, O my soul, and forget not all his benefits:

Who forgiveth all thine iniquities; who healeth all thy diseases;

Who redeemeth thy life from destruction; who crowneth thee with lovingkindness and tender mercies;

Who satisfieth thy mouth with good things; so that thy youth is renewed like the eagle's.

The Lord executeth righteousness and judgment for all that are oppressed.

He made known his ways unto Moses, his acts unto the children of Israel.

The Lord is merciful and gracious, slow to anger, and plenteous in mercy.

He will not always chide: neither will he keep his anger for ever.

He hath not dealt with us after our sins; nor rewarded us according to our iniquities.

For as the heaven is high above the earth, so great is his mercy toward them that fear him.

As far as the east is from the west, so far hath he removed our transgression from us.

Like as a father pitieth his children, so the Lord pitieth them that fear him.

For he knoweth our frame; he remembereth that we are dust.

As for man, his days are as grass: as a flower of the field, so he flourisheth.

For the wind passeth over it, and it is gone; and the place thereof shall know it no more.

But the mercy of the Lord is from everlasting to everlasting upon them that fear him, and his righteousness unto children's children;

159

To such as keep his covenant, and to those that remember his commandments to do them.

The Lord hath prepared his throne in the heavens; and his kingdom ruleth over all.

Bless the Lord, ye his angels, that excel in strength, that do his commandments, hearkening unto the voice of his word.

Bless ye the Lord, all ye his hosts; ye ministers of his, that do his pleasure.

Bless the Lord, all his works in all places of his dominion: bless the Lord, O my soul.

PSALM 103

DAY 246 TAOISM

International Altruism

Therefore, if a great kingdom humbles itself before a small kingdom, it shall make that small kingdom its prize. And if a small kingdom humbles itself before a great kingdom, it shall win over that great kingdom. Thus the one humbles itself in order to attain, the other attains because it is humble. If the great kingdom has no further desire than to bring men together and to nourish them, the small kingdom will have no further desire than to enter the service of the other. But in order that both may have their desire, the great one must learn humility.

TAO-TE-KING

DAY 247 BUDDHISM

Unprofitable Talk

Now at that time the brethren of the Band of Six had a habit of rising up in the night before it was dawn. Then, donning wooden slippers, they used to parade up and down in the open air, chattering in shrill loud tones, hawking and spitting, and talking all manner of idle babble, such as: talk about kings and robbers and ministers of state; talk about food, drink, clothes, beds, lodgings, flower-garlands, scents, kinsfolk, and carriages; about villages, suburbs, towns, provinces, women and soldiers; gossip of the

160

streets and wells, and tales of ghosts; all sorts of talk: about the world and the ocean; of things existent and nonexistent. And while so doing they trampled to death all sorts of insects. Moreover, they distracted the brethren from their meditation.

DIGHA NIKAYA

DAY 248 CHRISTIANITY

Of Anxiety

Anxiety is the greatest evil that can befall the soul, sin only excepted. The seditious and intestine troubles of a commonwealth ruin it completely and prevent it from being able to resist a foreign invasion. So also, when our heart is troubled and disturbed within itself, it loses the strength necessary to maintain the virtues it had acquired. At the same time it loses the means to resist the temptations of the enemy, who then uses his utmost efforts to fish, as they say, in troubled waters.

Anxiety proceeds from an inordinate desire of being delivered from the evil that we feel or of acquiring the good that we hope for. Yet there is nothing that tends more to increase evil and to prevent the enjoyment of good than inquietude and anxiety. Birds remain caught in nets and traps because when they find themselves ensnared, they eagerly flutter about and struggle to extricate themselves and in that way entangle themselves all the more. Whenever you are pressed with a desire to be freed from some evil or to obtain some good, before all else be careful both to settle your mind in repose and tranquillity and to compose your judgment and will. Then gently and meekly procure the accomplishment of your desire, taking in regular order the means that may be most convenient. When I say gently, I do not mean carelessly, but without hurry, trouble, or anxiety. Otherwise, instead of obtaining the effect you desire, you will mar all and embarrass yourself the more.

ST. FRANCIS DE SALES

The Forenoon

In the Name of God, the Merciful, the Compassionate
By the white forenoon
and the brooding night!
Thy Lord has neither forsaken thee nor hates thee
and the Last shall be better for thee than the First.
Thy Lord shall give thee, and thou shalt be satisfied.

Did He not find thee an orphan, and shelter thee?
Did He not find thee erring, and guide thee?
Did He not find thee needy, and suffice thee?

As for the orphan, do not oppress him,
and as for the beggar, scold him not;
and as for thy Lord's blessing, declare it.

THE KORAN

Thankfulness for God's Deliverance

I love the Lord, because he hath heard my voice and my supplications.

Because he hath inclined his ear unto me, therefore will I call upon him as long as I live.

The sorrows of death compassed me, and the pains of hell gat hold upon me: I found trouble and sorrow.

Then called I upon the name of the Lord; O Lord, I beseech thee, deliver my soul.

Gracious is the Lord, and righteous; yea, our God is merciful.

The Lord preserveth the simple: I was brought low, and he helped me.

Return unto thy rest, O my soul; for the Lord hath dealt bountifully with thee.

For thou hast delivered my soul from death, mine eyes from tears, and my feet from falling.

I will walk before the Lord in the land of the living.

I believed, therefore have I spoken: I was greatly afflicted:

I said in my haste, All men are liars.

What shall I render unto the Lord for all his benefits toward me?

I will take the cup of salvation, and call upon the name of the Lord.

I will pay my vows unto the Lord now in the presence of all his people.

Precious in the sight of the Lord is the death of his saints.

O Lord, truly I am thy servant: I am thy servant, and the son of thine handmaid: thou hast loosed my bonds.

I will offer to thee the sacrifice of thanksgiving, and will call upon the name of the Lord.

I will pay my vows unto the Lord now in the presence of all his people.

In the courts of the Lord's house, in the midst of thee, O Jerusalem. Praise ye the Lord.

PSALM 116

DAY 251   TAOISM
On Knowing When to Stop

Fame or one's own self, which does one love more?
One's own self or material goods, which has more worth?
Loss (of self) or possession (of goods), which is the greater evil?

Therefore: he who loves most spends most,
   He who hoards much loses much.
The contented man meets no disgrace;
Who knows when to stop runs into no danger—
He can long endure.

TAO-TE-KING

The Value of Understanding

Although a man can repeat a thousand stanzas, but understand not the meaning of the lines he repeats, this is not equal to the repetition of one sentence well understood, which is able when heard to control thought. To repeat a thousand words without understanding, what profit is there in this? But to understand one truth, and hearing it to act accordingly, this is to find deliverance. A man may be able to repeat many books, but if he cannot explain them what profit is there in this? But to explain one sentence of the Law and to walk accordingly, this is the way to find supreme wisdom.

DHAMMAPADA

A Night Prayer

Blessed art thou, O Lord our God, King of the universe, who makest the bands of sleep to fall upon mine eyes, and slumber upon my eyelids. May it be thy will, O Lord my God and God of my fathers, to suffer me to lie down in peace and to let me arise up again in peace. Let not my thoughts trouble me, nor evil dreams, nor evil fancies, but let my rest be perfect before thee. O lighten mine eyes lest I sleep the sleep of death, for it is thou who givest light to the apple of the eye. Blessed art thou, O Lord, who givest light to the whole world in thy glory.

BERAKOTH

Feelings Essential to Man

All men have a mind which cannot bear to see the sufferings of others. . . . My meaning may be illustrated thus: even nowadays, if men suddenly see a child about to fall into a well, they will without exception experience a feeling of alarm and distress.

From this case we may perceive that the feeling of commiseration is essential to man, that the feeling of shame and dislike is
essential to man, that the feeling of modesty and complaisance is
essential to man, and that the feeling of approving and disapproving is essential to man.

The feeling of commiseration is the principle of benevolence.
The feeling of shame and dislike is the principle of righteousness.
The feeling of modesty and complaisance is the principle of propriety. The feeling of approving and disapproving is the principle of knowledge.

From the want of benevolence and the want of wisdom will
ensue the entire absence of propriety and righteousness; he who
is in such a case must be the servant of other men. To be the
servant of men and yet ashamed of such servitude is like a bow-
maker's being ashamed to make bows, or an arrow-maker's being
ashamed to make arrows. If he be ashamed of his case, his best
course is to practice benevolence.

The man who would be benevolent is like the archer. The
archer adjusts himself and then shoots. If he misses, he does not
murmur against those who surpass him. He simply turns round
and seeks the cause of the failure in himself.

MENCIUS

DAY 255   CHRISTIANITY
The Pharisee and the Publican

And he spake this parable unto certain which trusted in themselves that they were righteous, and despised others: Two men
went up into the temple to pray; the one a Pharisee, and the other
a publican. The Pharisee stood and prayed thus with himself,
God, I thank thee, that I am not as other men are, extortioners,
unjust, adulterers, or even as this publican. I fast twice in the
week, I give tithes of all that I possess. And the publican, standing afar off, would not lift up so much as his eyes unto heaven,
but smote upon his breast, saying, God be merciful to me a
sinner. I tell you, this man went down to his house justified rather

165

than the other: for every one that exalteth himself shall be abased; and he that humbleth himself shall be exalted.

LUKE 18:9-14

DAY 256   HINDUISM

The Faithful Wife

In childhood must a father guard his daughter;
In youth the husband shields his wife; in age
A mother is protected by her sons—
Ne'er should a woman lean upon herself.

A faithful wife who wishes to attain
The heaven of her lord, must serve him here
As if he were a god, and ne'er do aught
To pain him, whatsoever be his state,
And even though devoid of every virtue.

She who in mind, speech, body, honours him,
Alive or dead, is called a virtuous wife.

Be it her duty to persevere with care
Her husband's substance; let her too be trusted
With its expenditure, with management
Of household property and furniture,
Of cooking and purveying daily food.

Let her be ever cheerful, skilled in all
Domestic work, and not too free in spending.

Drink, bad companions, absence from her lord,
Rambling about, unseasonable sleep,
Dwelling in others' houses, let her shun—
These are six things which tarnish woman's fame.

LAW OF MANU

Apparel

Excess in Apparel is another costly Folly. The very Trimming of the vain World would cloath all the naked one.

Chuse thy Cloaths by thine own Eyes, not another's. The more plain and simple they are, the better. Neither unshapely, nor fantastical; and for Use and Decency, and not for Pride.

If thou art clean and warm, it is sufficient; for more doth but rob the Poor, and please the Wanton.

It is said of the true Church, the King's Daughter is all glorious within. Let our Care therefore be of our Minds more than of our Bodies, if we would be of her Communion.

We are told with Truth, that Meekness and Modesty are the Rich and Charming Attire of the Soul: And the plainer the Dress, the more Distinctly, and with greater Lustre, their Beauty shines.

It is great Pity such Beauties are so rare, and those of Jezebel's Forehead are so common: Whose Dresses are Incentives to Lust; but Bars instead of Motives, to Love or Vertue.

WILLIAM PENN, *Some Fruits of Solitude*

The Proper Nature of an Offering

Magha, make offering, (he said),
But in so doing, cleanse thy heart
In all its ways. To the offerer
The offering is the help; by this
Supported, he doth then quit hate.

With passion gone and hate expelled,
Let him in boundless measure then
Quicken a heart of amity,
E'er day and night with zeal suffuse
All quarters to infinitude.

Who offers, Magha (he replied),
The offering threefold endowed,
He would make offerings prosperous
By giving to gift-worthy men;
And rightly minded, offering thus,
The ready almoner doth rise
Unto the world of Brahma, I say.

SUTTA NIPATA

DAY 259   CONFUCIANISM

Hypocrisy

A man of Ch'i had a wife and a concubine, and lived together
with them in his house. When the man went out, he was sure
to get himself well filled with meat and drink. The wife said to
the concubine one day, "When I ask him with whom he has
been eating and drinking, they are all men of wealth and rank.
And yet no men of distinction ever come here. I will spy out
where he goes." She got up early in the morning, and privately
followed him. All through the city there was nobody who stood
and talked with him. At last he came to those who were sacrificing
among the tombs outside the outer wall on the east, and begged
what they had left. Not being satisfied, he looked around him and
went to another party; and this was the way in which he got
himself satiated. His wife went home, and informed the concubine, saying, "It was to my husband that we looked up in
hopeful contemplation, and with whom our lot is cast for life;
and these are his ways." They reviled the man, and wept together
in the middle courtyard. In the meantime, the man, knowing
nothing of all this, came in with a jaunty air, carrying himself
proudly to them.

According to the view which a superior man takes of things,
as to the ways by which men seek for riches, honors, gain, and ad-
vancement, there are few of their wives and concubines who
might not be ashamed and weep together because of them.

MENCIUS

168

Children—The Gift of God

Except the Lord build the house, they labour in vain that build it: except the Lord keep the city, the watchman waketh but in vain.

It is vain for you to rise up early, to sit up late, to eat the bread of sorrows: for so he giveth his beloved sleep.

Lo, children are an heritage of the Lord: and the fruit of the womb is his reward.

As arrows are in the hand of a mighty man; so are children of the youth.

Happy is the man that hath his quiver full of them: they shall not be ashamed, but they shall speak with the enemies in the gate.

PSALM 127

The Danger of Overweening Success

Stretch [a bow] to the very full,
    And you will wish you had stopped in time.
Temper a [sword edge] to its very sharpest,
    And the edge will not last long.
When gold and jade fill your hall,
    You will not be able to keep them safe.
To be proud with wealth and honor
    Is to sow the seeds of one's own downfall.
Retire when your work is done,
    Such is Heaven's way.

TAO-TE-KING

The Peril of Wealth

And a certain ruler asked him, saying, Good Master, what shall I do to inherit eternal life? And Jesus said unto him, Why callest thou me good? none is good, save one, that is, God. Thou knowest the commandments, Do not commit adultery, Do not kill, Do not steal, Do not bear false witness, Honour thy father and thy mother. And he said, All these have I kept from my youth up. Now when Jesus heard these things, he said unto him, Yet lackest thou one thing: sell all that thou hast, and distribute unto the poor, and thou shalt have treasure in heaven: and come, follow me. And when he heard this, he was very sorrowful: for he was very rich. And when Jesus saw that he was very sorrowful, he said, How hardly shall they that have riches enter into the kingdom of God! For it is easier for a camel to go through a needle's eye, than for a rich man to enter into the kingdom of God. And they that heard it said, Who then can be saved? And he said, The things which are impossible with men are possible with God. Then Peter said, Lo, we have left all and followed thee. And he said unto them, Verily I say unto you, There is no man that hath left house, or parents, or brethren, or wife, or children, for the kingdom of God's sake, Who shall not receive manifold more in this present time, and in the world to come life everlasting.

LUKE 18:18-30

DAY 263   BUDDHISM
Sources of Suffering

When man is proud of birth
And purse and family,
And yet ashamed of kin:
A source of suffering that.

When man on woman dotes,
On drink and dice alike,
And all his savings wastes:
A source of suffering that.

Who, not content with his,
Is seen with others' wives,
Is seen with harlots too:
A source of suffering that.

When man, passed youth, doth wed
A maid with rounded breasts
Nor sleeps for jealousy:
A source of suffering that.

When woman or when man,
A spendthrift or a sot,
Is placed in sovran power:
A source of suffering that.

When born of noble clan,
A man is poor and craves
For much and longs to rule:
A source of suffering that.

These sufferings in the world
The wise discern, and blest
With vision Ariyan,
They seek the world of bliss.

SUTTA NIPATA

DAY 264   HINDUISM
The Companionship of Virtue

Single is every living creature born,
Single he passes to another world,
Single he eats the fruit of evil deeds,
Single, the fruit of good; and when he leaves
His body like a log or heap of clay
Upon the ground, his kinsmen walk away;
Virtue alone stays by him at the tomb
And bears him through the dreary trackless gloom.

LAW OF MANU

Religion

Religion is the fear of God, and its Demonstration is good works; and Faith is the Root of both: For without Faith we cannot please God, nor can we fear what we do not believe.

The Devils also believe and know abundance: But in this is the Difference, their Faith works not by Love, nor their Knowledge by Obedience; and therefore they are never the better for them. And if ours be such, we shall be of their Church, not of Christ's: For as the Head is, so must the Body be.

He was Holy, Humble, Harmless, Meek, Merciful, etc. when among us; to teach us what we should be, when he was gone. And yet he is among us still, and in us too, a living and perpetual Preacher of the same Grace, by his Spirit in our Consciences.

To be like Christ then, is to be a Christian. And regeneration is the only way to the Kingdom of God, which we pray for.

WILLIAM PENN, *Some Fruits of Solitude*

The Good General

He who by Tao purposes to help the ruler of men
Will oppose all conquest by force of arms.
For such things are wont to rebound.
Where armies are, thorns and brambles grow.
The raising of a great host
Is followed by a year of dearth.

Therefore a good general effects his purpose and stops.
    He dares not rely upon the strength of arms;
Effects his purpose and does not glory in it;
Effects his purpose and does not boast of it;
Effects his purpose and does not take pride in it;
    Effects his purpose as a regrettable necessity;
    Effects his purpose but does not love violence.
[For] things age after reaching their prime.

That [violence] would be against the Tao.
And he who is against the Tao perishes young.

TAO-TE-KING

DAY 267   CHRISTIANITY
The Duties of Christian Membership

Let love be without dissimulation. Abhor that which is evil;
cleave to that which is good. Be kindly affectioned one to another
with brotherly love; in honour preferring one another; Not slothful in business; fervent in spirit; serving the Lord; Rejoicing in
hope; patient in tribulation; continuing instant in prayer; Distribut-
ing to the necessity of saints; given to hospitality. Bless them
which persecute you; bless, and curse not. Rejoice with them that
do rejoice, and weep with them that weep. Be of the same mind
one toward another. Mind not high things, but condescend to
men of low estate. Be not wise in your own conceits. Recompense
to no man evil for evil. Provide things honest in the sight of all
men. If it be possible, as much as lieth in you, live peaceably with
all men. Dearly beloved, avenge not yourselves, but rather give
place unto wrath: for it is written, Vengeance is mine; I will repay, saith the Lord. Therefore if thine enemy hunger, feed him;
if he thirst, give him drink: for in so doing thou shalt heap coals
of fire on his head. Be not overcome of evil, but overcome evil
with good.

ROMANS 12:9-21

DAY 268   BUDDHISM
The Four Virtues

Who doth what seemly is and fit,
And on his back the burden bears
With vigor, he may riches find;
Speaking the truth he wins renown;
And friends by giving he will bind.
In this world and where life shall be
Thus will he lose all misery.

Whoso the layman's life doth seek
In pious faith and hath these four—
Veracity and self-control,
Steadfastness, generosity—
When passed away, he'll weep no more.

SAMYUTTA NIKAYA

DAY 269   AFRICAN RELIGION
Irony

A man has been beaten six times and is advised to be patient. What else is there for him to do?

When death is not ready to receive a man, it sends an expert physician at the right time.

Kindness shown to a hen is not lost. After a long time it gives a good meal.

It is the great God himself who drives away the flies from a tailless cow.

One who has planted a hundred pieces of yam, and says he planted two hundred, will have to eat his lies when the yam are finished.

YORUBA PROVERBS

DAY 270   JUDAISM
To Be a Man

Do not separate yourself from the congregation, and do not trust in yourself till the day of your death. Do not judge your friend until you find yourself in the same situation as he. Do not say, "I will study when I get some spare time," for you may never find time.

No boor fears sin, nor is the vulgar man pious. The shamefaced man is not apt to learn, nor the passionate to teach—nor is everyone wise who is always talking. In a place where there are no men, endeavor to be a man.

HILLEL

174

All Distinctions Pass Away

By anger, fear, and avarice deluded,
Men do not strive to understand themselves,
Nor gain self-knowledge. One is proud
Of rank, and plumes himself upon his birth,
Contemning those of low degree; another
Boasts of his riches, and disdains the poor;
Another vaunts his learning, and despising
Men of less wisdom, calls them fools; a fourth
Piquing himself upon his rectitude
Is quick to censure other people's faults
But when the high and low, the rich and poor,
The wise and foolish, worthy and unworthy,
Are borne to their last resting-place—the grave—
When all their troubles end in that last sleep,
And of their earthly bodies naught remains
But fleshless skeletons—can living men
Mark differences between them, or perceive
Distinctions in the dust of birth or form?
Since all are, therefore, levelled by the grave,
And all must sleep together in the earth—
Why, foolish mortals, do you wrong each other?

MAHABHARATA

A Temple Not Made by Hands

It was opened in me that God, who made the world, did not dwell in temples made with hands. This, at the first, seemed a strange word because both priests and people use to call their temples or churches, dreadful places, and holy ground, and the temples of God. But the Lord showed me, so that I did see clearly, that He did not dwell in these temples which men had commanded and set up, but in people's hearts; for both Stephen and

175

the Apostle Paul bore testimony that He did not dwell in temples made with hands, not even in that which He had once commanded to be built, since He put an end to it; but that His people were His temple, and He dwelt in them. This opened in me as I walked in the fields to my relations' house. And when I came there, they told me that Nathaniel Stephens the priest had been there, and told them he was afraid of me for going after new lights. And I smiled to myself, knowing what the Lord had opened in me concerning him and his brethren, but I told not my relations, who, though they saw beyond the priests, yet they went to hear them, and were grieved because I would not go also. But I brought them Scriptures, and told them there was an annointing within man to teach him, and that the Lord would teach His people Himself.

GEORGE FOX

DAY 273   ISLAM
God's Judgment

The Prophet's saying, "The Pen has dried," when you interpret it
   in its true sense, is a summons to the most important work of all.
If you do iniquity, you are damned: the Pen has dried on that.
   If you act righteously, you will eat the fruit of blessedness: the
   Pen has dried on that.
Is it conceivable that because of the Decree in eternity God
   should say, like a minister dismissed from office,
"The affair has gone out of My hands; 'tis vain to approach Me
   with entreaties"?
Nay, if your orisons exceed those of another by a single mite, that
   mite will be weighed in God's scales.

JALALU'L-DIN RUMI

DAY 274   CHRISTIANITY
The Foolishness of Preaching

For Christ sent me not to baptize, but to preach the gospel:
not with the wisdom of words, lest the cross of Christ should be

176

made of none effect. For the preaching of the cross is to them that perish foolishness; but unto us which are saved it is the power of God. For it is written, I will destroy the wisdom of the wise, and will bring to nothing the understanding of the prudent. Where is the wise? where is the scribe? where is the disputer of this world? hath not God made foolish the wisdom of this world? For after that in the wisdom of God the world by wisdom knew not God, it pleased God by the foolishness of preaching to save them that believe. For the Jews require a sign, and the Greeks seek after wisdom: But we preach Christ crucified, unto the Jews a stumbling-block, and unto the Greeks foolishness; But unto them which are called, both Jews and Greeks, Christ the power of God, and the wisdom of God. Because the foolishness of God is wiser than men; and the weakness of God is stronger than men. For ye see your calling, brethren, how that not many wise men after the flesh, not many mighty, not many noble, are called: But God hath chosen the foolish things of the world to confound the wise; and God hath chosen the weak things of the world to confound the things which are mighty; And base things of the world, and things which are despised, hath God chosen, yea, and things which are not, to bring to nought things that are; That no flesh should glory in his presence. But of him are ye in Christ Jesus, who of God is made unto us wisdom, and righteousness, and sanctification, and redemption: That, according as it is written, He that glorieth, let him glory in the Lord.

I CORINTHIANS I:17-31

DAY 275   HINDUISM

Virtue

Daily perform thy own appointed work
Unweariedly; and to obtain a friend—
A sure companion to the future world—
Collect a store of virtue like the ants
Who garner up their treasures into heaps;
For neither father, mother, wife, nor son,
Nor kinsman, will remain beside thee then,

177

When thou are passing to that other home—
Thy virtue will be thy only comrade.

LAW OF MANU

DAY 276   CONFUCIANISM
Responding to Nature

You glorify Nature and meditate on her:
Why not domesticate her and regulate her?

You obey Nature and sing her praise:
Why not control her course and use it?

You look on the seasons with reverence and await them:
Why not respond to them by seasonly activities?

You depend on things and marvel at them:
Why not unfold your own ability and transform them?

You meditate on what makes a thing a thing:
Why not so order things that you may not waste them?

You vainly seek the cause of things:
Why not appropriate and enjoy what they produce?

Therefore, I say: "To neglect man and speculate about Nature
Is to misunderstand the facts of the universe."

HSUN-TSE

DAY 277   CHRISTIANITY
God's Grandeur

The world is charged with the grandeur of God.
   It will flame out, like shining from shook foil;
   It gathers to a greatness, like the ooze of oil.
Crushed. Why do men then now not reck his rod?
Generations have trod, have trod, have trod;
   And all is seared with trade; bleared, smeared with toil;
   And wears man's smudge and shares man's smell: the soil
Is bare now, nor can foot feel, being shod.

And for all this, nature is never spent;
There lives the dearest freshness deep down things;
And though the last lights off the black West went
Oh, morning at the brown brink eastward, springs—
Because the Holy Ghost over the bent
World broods with warm breast and with ah! bright wings.

GERARD MANLEY HOPKINS

DAY 278   JUDAISM

Planting for Posterity

In his travels, Choni the Maagol once saw an old man planting a carob tree, and he asked him when he thought the tree
would bear fruit. "After seventy years," was the reply. "What?"
said Choni. "Do you expect to live seventy years and eat the
fruit of your labor?" "I did not find the world desolate when I entered it," said the old man, "and as my fathers planted for me before I was born, so I plant for those that will come after me."

TAANITH

DAY 279   TAOISM

Warning Against Interference

There are those who will conquer the world
And make of it [what they conceive or desire].
   I see that they will not succeed.
[For] the world is God's own Vessel
It cannot be made [by human interference].
   He who makes it spoils it.
   He who holds it loses it.
For: Some things go forward,
   Some things follow behind;
   Some blow hot,
   And some blow cold;
   Some are strong,
   And some are weak;

Some may break,
And some may fall.
Hence the Sage eschews excess,
   eschews extravagance,
   eschews pride.

TAO-TE-KING

HINDUISM

DAY 280

Good Deeds and Great Blessings

To injure none by thought or word or deed,
To give to others, and be kind to all—
This is the constant duty of the good.
High-minded men delight in doing good,
Without a thought of their own interest;
When they confer a benefit on others,
They reckon not on favors in return.

Two persons will hereafter be exalted
Above the heavens—the man with boundless power
Who yet forbears to use it indiscreetly,
And he who is not rich and yet can give.

Good words, good deeds, and beautiful expressions
A wise man ever culls from every quarter,
E'en as a gleaner gathers ears of corn.

To curb the tongue and moderate the speech,
Is held to be the hardest of all tasks.
The words of him who talks too volubly
Have neither substance nor variety.

MAHABHARATA

GREEK

DAY 281

The True God

 Homer and Hesiod have ascribed to the gods all things that are
a shame and disgrace among mortals, stealings and adulteries and

deceivings of one another. But mortals deem that the gods are begotten as they are, and have clothes like theirs, and voice and form. Yes, and if oxen and horses or lions had hands, and could paint with their hands, and produce works of art as men do, horses would paint the forms of the gods like horses, and oxen like oxen, and make their bodies in the image of their several kinds.

The Ethiopians make their gods black and snub-nosed; the Thracians say theirs have blue eyes and red hair. The gods have not revealed all things to men from the beginning, but by seeking they find in time what is better.

One god, the greatest among gods and men, is like mortals neither in form nor in thought. . . . He sees all over, thinks all over, and hears all over.

But without toil he sways all things by the thought of his mind.

And he abides always in the selfsame place, not moving at all; nor does it befit him to go about, now hither, now thither.

XENOPHANES

DAY 282 CHRISTIANITY

The Best Way of All

I may speak in tongues of men or of angels, but if I am without love, I am a sounding gong or a clanging cymbal. I may have the gift of prophecy, and know every hidden truth; I may have faith strong enough to move mountains; but if I have no love, I am nothing. I may dole out all I possess, or even give my body to be burnt, but if I have no love, I am none the better.

Love is patient; love is kind and envies no one. Love is never boastful, nor conceited, nor rude; never selfish, not quick to take offense. Love keeps no score of wrongs; does not gloat over other men's sins, but delights in the truth. There is nothing that love cannot face; there is no limit to its faith, its hope, and its endurance.

Love will never come to an end. Are there prophets? their work will be over. Are there tongues of ecstasy? they will cease. Is there knowledge? it will vanish away; for our knowledge and our

181

prophecy alike are partial, and the partial vanishes when wholeness comes. When I was a child, my speech, my outlook, and my thoughts were all childish. When I grew up, I had finished with childish things. Now we see only puzzling reflections in a mirror, but then we shall see face to face. My knowledge now is partial; then it will be whole, like God's knowledge of me. In a word, there are three things that last for ever: faith, hope, and love; but the greatest of them all is love.

I CORINTHIANS 13

DAY 283   AFRICAN RELIGION
Foresight and Consequences

If you think of nothing but the irritation of the itch, nothing will prevent you from scratching to the bone.

One who takes another to court does not think that the other man has his own statement to make.

The mad fellow rejoices on the death day of his mother. He does not know that he will suffer tomorrow.

The knife is destroying its own house, and thinks it is destroying only an old sheath.

After the man has been cured, he beats the doctor.

The man who always expects the return of his kindness is worse than the man who has shown none.

We do not do a good deed and then sit down with it.

To live with a humble person refreshes the mind.

He who admits his fault is not kept kneeling long.

YORUBA PROVERBS

DAY 284   JUDAISM
On Overcoming Self-pride

When Rabbi Shmelke came to Nikolsburg to assume his duties as Rabbi, he locked himself in a room and began to pace back and forth. One of the welcoming party overheard him repeating again and again the many forms of greeting he anticipated. When the welcome was concluded, the man confessed that he had overheard Rabbi Shmelke, and inquired if the Rabbi would explain his odd action.

Rabbi Shmelke said: "I dislike intensely honors which tend to self-pride; therefore I rehearsed to myself all the words of welcome. No one appreciates self-praise, and after becoming accustomed to these words of acclaim by frequent repetition, I no longer felt pride in hearing these very phrases uttered by the committee of welcome."

HASIDIC STORY

DAY 285   HINDUISM
The Nature of the Good

Praise not the goodness of the grateful man
Who acts with kindness to his benefactors.
He who does good to those who do him wrong
Alone deserves the epithet of good.

The misery a foolish man endures
In seeking riches, is a hundredfold
More grievous than the sufferings of him
Who strives to gain eternal blessedness.

The little-minded ask: Does this man belong
To our own family? The noble-hearted
Regard the human race as all akin.

PANCHATANTRA

DAY 286   CHRISTIANITY
Misplaced Zeal

Nothing spoils human Nature more than false Zeal. The *Good-nature* of an Heathen is more God-like than the furious *Zeal* of a Christian.

Our Fallibility and the Shortness of our Knowledge should make us peaceable and gentle: because I *may* be Mistaken, I *must*

183

not be dogmatical and confident, peremptory and imperious. I *will*
not break the certain Laws of Charity, for a doubtful Doctrine or
of uncertain Truth.

BENJAMIN WHICHCOTE

DAY 287   TAOISM
Praise and Blame

"Favor and disgrace cause one dismay;
What we value and what we fear are within our Self."

What does this mean:
"Favor and disgrace cause one dismay"?
Those who receive a favor from above
  Are dismayed when they receive it,
  And dismayed when they lose it.

What does this mean:
"What we value and what we fear are within our Self"?
We have fears because we have a self.
When we do not regard that self as self,
What have we to fear?

Therefore he who values the world as his self
  May then be entrusted with the government of the world;
And he who loves the world as his self—
  The world may then be entrusted to his care.

TAO-TE-KING

DAY 288   HINDUISM
The Relativity of Experience

A sage was lying in a deep trance by a roadside. A thief passing by, saw him, and thought to himself, "This fellow, lying
here, is a thief. He has been breaking into some house by night,
and now sleeps exhausted. The police will very soon be here to
catch him. So let me escape in time." Thus thinking, he ran away.

Soon a drunkard came upon the sage, and said, "Hallo! you've

184

fallen into the ditch by taking a drop too much. I am steadier than you, and am not going to tumble."

Last of all came a sage, and understanding that a great sage was in a trance, he sat down, and touched him, and began gently to rub his holy feet.

RAMAKRISHNA

DAY 289   SIKHISM
At the Gate of the Lord

They who please God are good; what more can be said?
They in whose heart God is contained possess wisdom, honor, and
    wealth.
What need is there of praising them? What further decoration
    can they obtain?
Nanak, they who are beyond God's favoring glance love not
    charity or His Name.

NANAK

DAY 290   CHRISTIANITY
Recipients of Grace

We then, as workers together with him, beseech you also that ye receive not the grace of God in vain. (For he saith, I have heard thee in a time accepted, and in the day of salvation have I succoured thee: behold, now is the accepted time; behold, now is the day of salvation.) Giving no offence in any thing, that the ministry be not blamed: But in all things approving ourselves as the ministers of God, in much patience, in afflictions, in necessities, in distresses, in stripes, in imprisonments, in tumults, in labours, in watchings, in fastings; by pureness, by knowledge, by longsuffering, by kindness, by the Holy Ghost, by love unfeigned, by the word of truth, by the power of God, by the armour of righteousness on the right hand and on the left, by honour and dishonour, by evil report and good report: as deceivers, and yet true; as unknown, and yet well known; as dying, and, behold, we live; as chastened, and not killed; as sorrowful, yet alway re-

185

joicing; as poor, yet making many rich; as having nothing, and yet possessing all things.

O ye Corinthians, our mouth is open unto you, our heart is enlarged. Ye are not straitened in us, but ye are straitened in your own bowels. Now for a recompence in the same, (I speak as unto my children,) be ye also enlarged. Be ye not unequally yoked together with unbelievers: for what fellowship hath righteousness with unrighteousness? and what communion hath light with darkness? And what concord hath Christ with Belial? or what part hath he that believeth with an infidel? And what agreement hath the temple of God with idols? For ye are the temple of the living God; as God hath said, I will dwell in them, and walk in them; and I will be their God, and they shall be my people. Wherefore come out from among them, and be ye separate, saith the Lord, and touch not the unclean thing; and I will receive you, and will be a Father unto you, and ye shall be my sons and daughters, saith the Lord Almighty.

II CORINTHIANS 6:1-18

DAY 291   CONFUCIANISM
Confucius and the Children

Confucius was traveling east and met two children arguing with one another. He asked them what they were arguing about, and one child said, "I say the sun is nearer to us in the morning and farther away from us at noon, and he says the sun is farther away from us in the morning and nearer to us at noon." One child said, "When the sun begins to come up, it is big like a carriage cover, and at noon it is like a dinner plate. So it must be farther away when it looks smaller, and nearer us when it looks bigger." The other child said, "When the sun comes up, the air is very cool, but at noon it burns like hot soup. So it must be nearer when it is hot and farther away when it is cool." Confucius could not decide who was right, and the children laughed at him and said, "Whoever said that you were a wise guy?"

LIEHTSE

186

Though He Slay Me

Now I submit me to thy will,
Whether thou save or whether kill;
Keep thou me near or send me hence,
Or plunge me in the war of sense.

Thee in my ignorance I sought,
Of true devotion knowing nought.
Little could I, a dullard, know,
Myself the lowest of the low.

My mind I cannot steadfast hold;
My senses wander uncontrolled.
Ah, I have sought and sought for peace.
In vain; for me there's no release.

Now bring I thee a faith complete
And lay my life before thy feet.
Do thou, O God, what seemeth best;
In thee, in thee alone is rest.

In thee I trust, and, hapless wight,
Cling to thy skirts with all my might.
My strength is spent, I, Tuka say;
Now upon thee this task I lay.

TUKARAM

The Nature of Love

May creatures all abound
In weal and peace; may all
be blessed with peace always;
all creatures weak or strong,
all creatures great and small;

Creatures unseen or seen,
dwelling afar or near,
born or awaiting birth,
—may all be blessed with peace!

Let none cajole or flout
his fellows anywhere;
let none wish others harm
in dudgeon or in hate.

Just as with her own life
a mother shields from hurt
her own, her only, child—
let all-embracing thoughts
for all that lives be thine,

An all-embracing love
for all the universe
in all its heights and depths
and breadth, unstinted love,
unmarred by hate within,
not rousing enmity.

So, as you stand or walk,
or sit, or lie, reflect
with all your might on this;
—'tis deemed "a state divine."

                              SUTTA NIPATA

DAY 294   CHRISTIANITY
The Mirror of Mortality

Draw near, fond man, and dress thee by this glass,
Mark how thy bravery and big looks must pass
Into corruption, rottenness and dust;
The frail supporters which betray'd thy trust.
O weigh in time thy last and loathsome state,
To purchase heav'n for tears is no hard rate.
Our glory, greatness, wisdom, all we have,

If misemployed, but add hell to the grave:
Only a fair redemption of evil times
Finds life in death, and buries all our crimes.

HENRY VAUGHAN, The Mount of Olives

DAY 295   CHRISTIANITY
The Example of Christ

He set forth in Himself patterns of both lives, that is, the active and the contemplative, united together. For the contemplative life differs very much from the active. But our Redeemer by coming incarnate, while He gave a pattern of both, united both in Himself. For when He wrought miracles in the city, and yet continued all night in prayer on the mountain, He gave His faithful ones an example, not to neglect, through love of contemplation, the care of their neighbors, nor again to abandon contemplative pursuits, from being too immoderately engaged in the care of their neighbors; but so to keep together their mind, in applying it to the two cases, that the love of their neighbor might not interfere with the love of God, nor again the love of God cast out, because it transcends, the love of their neighbor.

ST. GREGORY THE GREAT

DAY 296   HINDUISM
The All-Filling God

Place has no power His presence can imprison,
    Boundless Bliss, all-filling Splendour,
  That, in its infinite fulness of loving grace,
    Foldeth the worlds that are, all things;
Grace that in graciousness willeth all life to lie
    In Him the Life of life's essence:
  Measureless by the mind, by speech unsearchable;
    Claim and the contest of all creeds;

189

Ways which bewilder the warring religions He
Taketh, none guessing His greatness.
He is the only Almighty, Eternal One,
Being beatific, Bliss He.
Praise Him on whom never night of forgetting falls
Dawneth no day of remembering;
Who is yet knowable, imaged in all we see,
In the still sweep of His Silence.

TAYUMANAVAR

DAY 297 CHRISTIANITY

On Bearing Burdens

Brethren, if a man be overtaken in a fault, ye which are spiritual, restore such an one in the spirit of meekness; considering thyself, lest thou also be tempted. Bear ye one another's burdens, and so fulfil the law of Christ. For if a man think himself to be something, when he is nothing, he deceiveth himself. But let every man prove his own work, and then shall he have rejoicing in himself alone, and not in another. For every man shall bear his own burden. Let him that is taught in the word communicate unto him that teacheth in all good things. Be not deceived; God is not mocked: for whatsoever a man soweth, that shall he also reap. For he that soweth to his flesh shall of the flesh reap corruption; but he that soweth to the Spirit shall of the Spirit reap life everlasting. And let us not be weary in well doing: for in due season we shall reap, if we faint not. As we have therefore opportunity, let us do good unto all men, especially unto them who are of the household of faith.

GALATIANS 6:1-10

DAY 298 CONFUCIANISM

Human-heartedness

The disciple Tsai Yu used to sleep during the day. The Master said, "Rotten wood is no good for carving. . . . What is the use of reproving him? . . . In the beginning I used to listen to what people said and trust them to act. Now I both listen to what they say and observe what they do. It was my experience with Tsai Yu which made me change. So! I have never seen any one who could see his own faults and press the charge home in his own breast. I have never seen a man who was really resolute."

Someone said that there was Shen Ch'eng, to which the Master replied, "Ch'eng! Why, he is all desires. How could he be resolute? For my part I have never seen anyone with a real passion for human-heartedness and a real hatred of what is inhuman. A man with a real passion for human-heartedness will not put anything above it. A man with a real hatred of what is inhuman will become human-hearted to the extent that he will not deliberately have anything inhuman affecting his self. Are there any who are able to devote their strength for a single day to being human-hearted? I have never seen any. [Nevertheless] I have never seen any who had not the strength to achieve this.

"Is human-heartedness something remote? If I want to be human-hearted, behold, human-heartedness has arrived."

ANALECTS

DAY 299   JUDAISM

On Being Particular

Rabbi Moshe Leib of Sasov once gave his last coin to a man of evil reputation. His students reproached him for it. Whereupon he replied: "Shall I be more particular than God, who gave the coin to me?"

HASIDIC STORY

DAY 300   CHRISTIANITY

For Forgiveness

Wilt Thou forgive that sin where I begun,
 Which was my sin, though it were done before?
Wilt Thou forgive that sin, through which I run

And do run still, though still I do deplore?
　　When thou hast done, Thou has not done;
　　　For I have more.

Wilt Thou forgive that sin which I have won
　　Others to sin, and made my sins their door?
Wilt Thou forgive that sin which I did shun
　　A year or two, but wallowed in a score?
　　When Thou hast done, Thou hast not done;
　　　For I have more.

I have a sin of fear, that when I have spun
　　My last thread, I shall perish on the shore:
But swear by thyself, that at my death Thy Son
　　Shall shine as He shines now and heretofore;
　　And, having done that, Thou hast done;
　　　I fear no more.

JOHN DONNE

DAY 301　　　　　　　　　　　　　　　　　　　BUDDHISM

The Mark of Kindred

. . . Behold the grass and trees!
They reason not, yet they possess the mark
After their kind: for kinds indeed divide.
Consider then the beetles, moths, and ants:
They after their kind too possess the mark . . .
And so four-footed creatures, great and small . . .
The reptiles, snakes, the long-backed animals . . .
Fish and pond-feeders, water denizens . . .
Birds and the winged creatures, fowls o'er the air,
They and their kind all possess the mark;
For kinds divide. Each after his kind bears
His mark: in man there is not manifold,
Not in the hair or head or ears or eyes,
Not in the mouth or nose or lips or brows,
Not in the throat, hips, belly or the back,
Not in the rump, sex-organs or the breast,

Not in the hands or feet, fingers or nails,
Not in the legs or thighs, colour or voice,
Is mark that forms his kind as in all else.
Nothing unique is in men's bodies found:
The difference in men is nominal.

SUTTA NIPATA

DAY 302   HINDUISM
Reflections on Life

No sacred lore can save the hypocrite,
Though he employ it craftily, from hell;
When his end comes, his pious texts take wing,
Like fledglings eager to forsake their nest.

Some who are wealthy perish in their youth,
While others who are fortuneless and needy,
Attain a hundred years; the prosperous man
Who lives, oft lacks the power to enjoy his wealth.

MAHABHARATA

DAY 303   TAOISM
Water

The best of men is like water;
    Water benefits all things
    And does not compete with them.
It dwells in [the lowly] places that all disdain—
    Wherein it comes near to the Tao.

In his dwelling, [the Sage] loves the [lowly] earth;
In his heart, he loves what is profound;
In his relations with others, he loves kindness;
In his words, he loves sincerity;
In government, he loves peace;
In business affairs, he loves ability;

In his actions, he loves choosing the right time.
        It is because he does not contend
        That he is without reproach.

TAO-TE-KING

DAY 304   ZOROASTRIANISM
Good Deeds Endure

Seek ye for a store of good deeds, O Zarathustra, men and
women! For a store of good deeds is full of salvation, O Zarathustra! For the ox turns to dust, the horse turns to dust; silver and
gold turn to dust, the valiant strong man turns to dust; the bodies
of all men mingle with the dust. What do not mingle with the
dust are confessions (Ashem-Vohu) which a man recites in this
world and his almsgiving to the holy and righteous.

AOGEMADAECHA

DAY 305   CHRISTIANITY
Renewal in the Spirit

And be renewed in the spirit of your mind; and . . . put on
the new man, which after God is created in righteousness and
true holiness. Wherefore putting away lying, speak every man
truth with his neighbour: for we are members one of another. Be
ye angry, and sin not: let not the sun go down upon your wrath:
Neither give place to the devil. Let him that stole steal no more:
but rather let him labour, working with his hands the thing
which is good, that he may have to give to him that needeth. Let
no corrupt communication proceed out of your mouth, but that
which is good to the use of edifying, that it may minister grace
unto the hearers. And grieve not the holy Spirit of God, whereby
ye are sealed unto the day of redemption. Let all bitterness, and
wrath, and anger, and clamour, and evil speaking, be put away
from you, with all malice: And be ye kind one to another, tender-
hearted, forgiving one another, even as God for Christ's sake hath
forgiven you.

EPHESIANS 4:23-32

194

The Intoxication of Pride

Once there was a lion named Durdanta ("Hard-to-tame"), who was always killing the other animals on Mount Mandara. Finally all the animals gathered together and petitioned the lion: "Your Majesty, why are you slaughtering us? We will daily furnish you with a single beast for your dinner as a gift."

"If that is agreeable to you," said the lion, "then so be it." From then on, every day he habitually fed upon the single beast that was provided.

Now one day an old rabbit's turn came, and the rabbit thought to himself, "Out of fear, one pretends humility in the hope of being spared. But if I have to die, why should I cringe before the lion? I will take my time about going to him."

When he arrived, the lion was enraged with hunger. "What took you so long?" he howled.

"It was not my fault," answered the rabbit. "On the road I was stopped by another lion. I promised him that I would return, and he allowed me to come and tell you."

Durdanta angrily exclaimed, "Take me along and show me where the scoundrel is!" They set forth and came to a deep well. Pointing to the water in it, the rabbit said, "Come here, my lord, and see." Glimpsing his own image reflected there, he pounced on it and was drowned.

Thus was a lion, intoxicated with pride, defeated by a clever rabbit. He who has sense has strength, but where is a fool's strength?

HITOPADESA

Of Endurance in Faith

When I consider how my light is spent
　　Ere half my days in this dark world and wide,
　　And that one talent which is death to hide

195

Lodged with me useless, though my soul more bent
To serve therewith my Maker, and present
My true account, lest He returning chide;
"Doth God exact day-labour, light denied?"
I fondly ask. But Patience, to prevent
That murmur, soon replies, "God doth not need
Either man's work or his own gifts. Who best
Bear his mild yoke, they serve him best. His state
Is kingly: thousands at his bidding speed,
And post o'er land and ocean without rest;
They also serve who only stand and wait."

JOHN MILTON

DAY 308   CONFUCIANISM

Humanism

Confucius said, "It is man that makes truth great, and not truth that makes man great. Truth may not depart from human nature. If what is regarded as truth departs from human nature, it may not be regarded as truth."

Tselu asked about the worship of the celestial and earthly spirits. Confucius said, "We don't know yet how to serve men. How can we know about serving the spirits?"

"What about death?" was the next question, and Confucius said, "We don't know yet about life. How can we know about death?"

A certain stable was burned down. On returning from the court, Confucius asked, "Was any man hurt?" And he did not ask about the horses.

CONFUCIUS

DAY 309   HINDUISM

Priorities

'Tis right to sacrifice an individual
For a whole household, and a family

For a whole village, and a village even
For a whole country's good; but for one's self
And one's own soul, one should give up the world.

HITOPADESA

The Duty of Work

For even when we were with you, this we commanded you, that if any would not work, neither should he eat. For we hear that there are some which walk among you disorderly, working not at all, but are busybodies. Now them that are such we command and exhort by our Lord Jesus Christ, that with quietness they work, and eat their own bread. But ye, brethren, be not weary in well doing. And if any man obey not our word by this epistle, note that man, and have no company with him, that he may be ashamed. Yet count him not as an enemy, but admonish him as a brother.

II THESSALONIANS 3:10-15

Nature and Instruction

Now we know that things which are difficult are not essential; but that things which are essential have been graciously made easy of attainment by God. Wherefore Democritus well says that "nature and instruction" are like each other. And we have briefly assigned the cause. For instruction harmonizes man, and by harmonizing makes him natural; and it is no matter whether one was made such as he is by nature, or transformed by time and education. The Lord has furnished both: that which is by creation, and that which is by creating again and renewal through the covenant.

CLEMENT OF ALEXANDRIA

The Knowledge of God

The God of Christians is a God who makes the soul perceive that He is its only good, that its only rest is in Him, its only joy in loving Him, who makes it at the same time abhor the obstacles which withhold it from loving Him with all its strength. Its two hindrances, self-love and lust, are insupportable to it. Thus God makes it perceive that the root of self-love destroys it, and that He alone can heal.

The knowledge of God without that of our wretchedness creates pride. The knowledge of our wretchedness without that of God creates despair. The knowledge of Jesus Christ is the middle way, because in Him we find both God and our wretchedness.

BLAISE PASCAL

God's Love and Care

No need to order a mother to love her child!

The child is there, and in need, that is all:
The love in her heart goes forth, and fulfills all
    his need:

Our God, so little we know of Thy secret nature,
Yet this much we know—
Thou art not less loving, less eager to help thy
    children,
Than a mortal mother.

Weak and foolish we are,
How can a mortal mother keep her child safe
    beyond death?

Yet Thou art able to save to the utmost,
Both here in this life, and beyond:

Thou art Master of Death and of Time:
And Thy love is wider and deeper—
O sovereign, ineffable Truth—
Thy love is wider and deeper, than the love of
the best earthly mother.

TUKARAM

DAY 314 TAOISM

The Riches of Innocence

Who is rich in character
Is like a child.
  No poisonous insects sting him,
  No wild beasts attack him,
  And no birds of prey pounce upon him.
His bones are soft, his sinews tender, yet his grip is
    strong.
Not knowing the union of male and female, yet his
    organs are complete,
  Which means his vigor is unspoiled.
Crying the whole day, yet his voice never runs hoarse,
  Which means his [natural] harmony is perfect.
To know harmony is to be in accord with the eternal,
[And] to know eternity is called discerning.
[But] to improve upon life is called an ill-omen;
To let go the emotions through impulse is called
    assertiveness.
[For] things age after reaching their prime;
That [assertiveness] would be against Tao.
And he who is against Tao perishes young.

TAO-TE-KING

DAY 315 CHRISTIANITY

Doers of the Word

But be ye doers of the word and not hearers only, deceiving
your own selves. For if any be a hearer of the word, and not a

doer, he is like unto a man beholding his natural face in a glass: For he beholdeth himself, and goeth his way, and straightway forgetteth what manner of man he was. But whoso looketh into the perfect law of liberty, and continueth therein, he being not a forgetful hearer, but a doer of the work, this man shall be blessed in his deed. If any man among you seem to be religious, and bridleth not his tongue, but deceive his own heart, this man's religion is vain. Pure religion and undefiled before God and the Father is this, To visit the fatherless and widows in their affliction, and to keep himself unspotted from the world.

JAMES 1:22-27

DAY 316   HINDUISM
Undiscerned Good Actions

> Just as the track of birds that cleave the air
> Is not discerned, nor yet the path of fish
> That skim the water, so the course of those
> Who do good actions, is not always seen.

MAHABHARATA

DAY 317   CHRISTIANITY
The Canticle of the Creatures

O most high, almighty, good Lord God: to thee belong praise, glory, honour, and all blessing!

Praisèd be my Lord God, with all His creatures: and specially our brother the sun, who brings us the day, and who brings us the light!

Fair is he, and shining with a very great splendour: O Lord, to us he signifies Thee.

Praisèd be my Lord for our sister the moon, and for the stars, the which He has set clear and lovely in heaven.

Praisèd be my Lord for our brother the wind: and for air and cloud, calms, and all weather, by the which Thou upholdest in life all creatures.

200

Praisèd be my Lord for our sister water, who is very service-able unto us, and humble and precious and clean.

Praisèd be my Lord for our brother fire, through whom thou givest us light in the darkness; and he is bright and pleasant and very mighty and strong.

Praisèd be my Lord for our mother the earth, the which doth sustain us and keep us, and bringeth forth divers fruits, and flowers of many colours, and grass.

Praisèd be my Lord for all those who pardon one another for His love's sake, and who endure weakness and tribulation.

Blessed are they who peaceably shall endure, for thou, O most Highest, shalt give them a crown.

Praisèd be my Lord for our sister the death of the body from whom no man escapeth. Woe to him who dieth in mortal sin. Blessed are they who are found walking by thy most holy will.

Praise ye and bless ye the Lord, and give thanks unto Him, and serve Him with great humility.

ST. FRANCIS OF ASSISI

DAY 318   TAOISM

The Nature of Tao

When the superior scholar is told of Tao,
He works hard to practice it.
When the middling scholar is told of Tao,
It seems that sometimes he keeps it and sometimes he loses it.
When the inferior scholar is told of Tao,
He laughs aloud at it.
If it were not laughed at, it would not be sufficient to be Tao.
Therefore the proverb says:
"Tao in enlightenment seems obscure;
Tao in progress seems regressive;
Tao in its straightness seems rugged.
The highest virtue seems like a valley;
The purest white seems discolored;
The most magnificent virtue seems insufficient;
The solidest virtue seems frail;

The simplest nature seems changeable;
The greatest square has no angles;
The largest vessel is never complete;
The loudest sound can scarcely be heard;
The biggest form cannot be visualized.
Tao, while hidden, is nameless."
Yet it is Tao alone that is good at imparting and completing.

TAO-TE-KING

DAY 319   ZOROASTRIANISM
Avoid Becoming Presumptuous

Do not become presumptuous through worldly happiness, for such happiness is like a rain cloud, which cannot be warded off; the hill does not shield you from the rain.

Do not become presumptuous through worldly wealth, for in the end you must leave it all behind.

Do not become presumptuous through ancestry or connections with the great, for in the end you must trust in your own deeds.

Do not become presumptuous through life, for death comes to you at last and what is perishable falls away.

MENOG-I-KHRAD

DAY 320   CHRISTIANITY
Keeping the Law Whole

Hath not God chosen the poor of this world rich in faith, and heirs of the kingdom which he hath promised to them that love him? But ye have despised the poor. Do not rich men oppress you, and draw you before the judgment seats? Do not they blaspheme that worthy name by the which ye are called? If ye fulfil the royal law according to the scripture, Thou shalt love thy neighbour as thyself, ye do well: But if ye have respect to persons, ye commit sin, and are convinced of the law as transgressors. For whosoever shall keep the whole law, and yet offend in one point, he is guilty of all.

JAMES 2:5-10

202

The Fruit of Iniquity

Neither a man who lives unrighteously,
　　Nor he who acquires wealth by telling falsehoods,
Nor he who always delights in doing injury,
　　Ever attains happiness in this world.

Though suffering in consequence of his righteousness,
　　Let one never turn his heart to unrighteousness,
For he will see the speedy overthrow
　　Of unrighteous wicked men.

Unrighteousness practiced in this world
　　Does not at once produce its fruit, like a cow;
But, advancing slowly, it cuts off
　　The root of him who committed it.

If the punishment falls not on the offender himself,
　　It falls on his sons;
If not on the sons,
　　At least on the grandsons.

But an iniquity, once committed, never fails
　　To produce fruit to him who wrought it.
He prospers for a while through unrighteousness;
　　Then he gains great good fortune;
Next he conquers his enemies;
　　But at last he perishes, branch and root.

LAW OF MANU

The Thankful Spirit

If anyone would tell you the shortest, surest way to all happiness and all perfection, he must tell you to make a rule to yourself, to thank and praise God for everything that happens to you. For it is certain that whatever seeming calamity happens to you, if you thank and praise God for it, you turn it into a blessing. Could you therefore work miracles, you could not do more for yourself, than by this thankful spirit, for it heals with a word speaking, and turns all that it touches into happiness.

And although this be the highest temper that you can aim at, though it be the noblest sacrifice that the greatest saint can offer unto God, yet it is not tied to any time or place or great occasion, but is always in your power, and may be the exercise of every day. For the common events of every day are sufficient to discover and exercise this temper, and may plainly show you how far you are governed in all your actions by this thankful spirit.

WILLIAM LAW

DAY 323   TAOISM
The Tenderness of Life

Man when living is soft and tender; when dead he is hard and tough. All animals and plants when living are tender and fragile; when dead they become withered and dry. Therefore it is said: the hard and tough are parts of death; the soft and tender are parts of life. This is the reason why the soldiers when they are too tough cannot carry the day; the tree when it is too tough will break. The position of the strong and great is low, and the position of the weak and tender is high.

TAO-TE-KING

DAY 324   GREEK
The Nature of Death

"We shall see that there is great reason to hope that death is good; for one of two things—either death is a state of . . . utter unconsciousness, or as men say, there is a change and migration of the soul from this world to another. Now if you suppose that there is no consciousness, but a sleep like the sleep of him who is undisturbed even by dreams. . . . I say that to die is gain; for eternity is then only a single night. But if death is a journey to another place, and there, as men say, all the dead abide, what good . . . can be greater than this? . . . What would not a man give if he might converse with Orpheus and Hesiod and Homer? . . . What infinite delight would there be in conversing with them and asking them questions! In another world they do not put a man to death for asking questions: assuredly not. . . .

"Wherefore, O judges, be of good cheer about death and know of a certainty, that no evil can happen to a good man, either in life or after death. He and his are not neglected by the gods. . . . For which reason, also, I am not angry with my condemners, or with my accusers; they have done me no harm, although they did not mean to do me any good; and for this I may gently blame them.

". . . The hour of departure has arrived, and we go our ways —I to die and you to live. Which is better God only knows."

PLATO, Apology

DAY 325   CHRISTIANITY

Faith and Works

What doth it profit, my brethren, though a man say he hath faith, and have not works? can faith save him? If a brother or sister be naked, and destitute of daily food, and one of you say unto them, Depart in peace, be ye warmed and filled; notwithstanding ye give them not those things which are needful to the body; what doth it profit? Even so faith, if it hath not works, is dead, being alone. Yea, a man may say, Thou hast faith, and I have works; shew me thy faith without thy works, and I will shew thee my faith by my works. Thou believest that there is one God; thou doest well: the devils also believe, and tremble. But wilt thou know, O vain man, that faith without works is dead? Was not Abraham our father justified by works, when he had offered Isaac his son upon the altar? Seest thou how faith wrought with his works, and by works was faith made perfect? And the scripture was fulfilled which saith, Abraham believed God, and it was imputed unto him for righteousness: and he was called the Friend of God. Ye see then how that by works a man is justified, and not by faith only. Likewise also was not Rahab the harlot justified by works, when she had received the messengers, and had sent them out another way? For as the body without the spirit is dead, so faith without works is dead also.

JAMES 2:14-26

DAY 326   ANTI-CONFUCIANISM
The Will of Heaven

Now, what does Heaven desire and what does it abominate? Heaven desires righteousness and abominates unrighteousness. . . . But how do we know Heaven desires righteousness and abominates unrighteousness? For with righteousness the world lives and without it the world dies; with it the world becomes rich and without it the world becomes poor; with it the world becomes orderly and without it the world becomes chaotic. And Heaven likes to have the world live and dislikes to have it die, likes to have it rich and dislikes to have it poor, and likes to have it orderly and dislikes to have it disorderly. Therefore we know Heaven desires righteousness and abominates unrighteousness.

MOTSE

DAY 327   CHRISTIANITY
The Time of Prayer

Brother Lawrence had found such an advantage in walking in the presence of God, it was natural for him to recommend it earnestly to others; but his example was a stronger inducement than any arguments he could propose. His very countenance was edifying; such a sweet and calm devotion appearing in it, as could not but affect the beholders. And it was observed, that in the greatest hurry of business in the kitchen, he still preserved his recollection and heavenly mindedness. He was never hasty nor loitering, but did each thing in its season, with an even, uninterrupted composure and tranquillity of spirit. "The time of business," said he, "does not with me differ from the time of prayer; and in the noise and clatter of my kitchen, while several persons are at the same time calling for different things, I possess God in as great tranquillity as if I were upon my knees at the Blessed Sacrament."

BROTHER LAWRENCE

DAY 328   HINDUISM
Good Words

Good words, good deeds, and beautiful expressions
A wise man ever culls from every quarter,
Even as a gleaner gathers ears of corn.

To curb the tongue and moderate the speech
Is held to be the hardest of all tasks.
The words of him who talks too volubly
Have neither substance nor variety.

MAHABHARATA

DAY 329   SIKHISM
Returning Good for Evil

It is characteristic of a tree that it returns good for evil. It lets a man sit in its shade even though he has lopped its branches. When you throw turf at it, it gives you its fruit. Carve it into a boat and it protects you from drowning.

Those who are perverse and do not have the tree's generosity and endurance, do not get any fruits in life; but for the faithful, there are many fruits. To return good for good is the way of the world; but the way of the Guru is to return good for evil.

BHAI GUR DAS

207

God's Love for His Children

Whosoever is born of God doth not commit sin; for his seed remaineth in him: and he cannot sin, because he is born of God. In this the children of God are manifest, and the children of the devil: whosoever doeth not righteousness is not of God, neither he that loveth not his brother. For this is the message that ye heard from the beginning, that we should love one another. . . . We know that we have passed from death unto life, because we love the brethren. He that loveth not his brother abideth in death. Whosoever hateth his brother is a murderer: and ye know that no murderer hath eternal life abiding in him. Hereby perceive we the love of God, because he laid down his life for us: and we ought to lay down our lives for the brethren.

I JOHN 3:9-11, 14-16

Practice Makes Right

Repeated sin destroys the understanding,
And he whose reason is impaired, repeats
His sins. The constant practicing of virtue
Strengthens the mental faculties, and he
Whose judgment stronger grows, acts always right.

MAHABHARATA

Always Autumn in Heaven

God made sun and moon to distinguish seasons, and day and night, and we cannot have the fruits of the earth but in their seasons: but God hath made no decree to distinguish the seasons of his mercies; in paradise the fruits were ripe, the first minute, and in heaven it is always autumn, his mercies are ever in their maturity. We ask *panem quotidianum,* our daily bread, and God never says you should have come yesterday, he never says you must come again tomorrow, but "today if you will hear his voice," today he will hear you. If some king of the earth hath so large an extent of dominion in north and south, as that he hath winter and summer together in his dominions, so large an extent east and west, as that he hath day and night together in his dominions, much more hath God mercy and judgment together: . . . though . . . thou have been benighted till now, wintered and frozen, clouded and eclipsed, damped and benumbed, smothered and stupefied till now, how God comes to thee, not as in the dawning of the day, not as in the bud of spring, but as the sun at noon to illustrate all shadows, as the sheaves in harvest, to fill all penuries, all occasions invite his mercies, and all times are his seasons.

JOHN DONNE

DAY 333   JUDAISM

Equality

A single man was created for the sake of peace among mankind, that none should say to his fellow, "My father was greater than your father."

T. J. SANHEDRIN

DAY 334   TAOISM

Double Enlightenment

A good traveller leaves no track;
A good speaker leaves no error;
A good reckoner needs no counter;
A good closer needs no bars or bolts,
And yet it is impossible to open after him.
A good fastener needs no cords or knots,
And yet it is impossible to untie after him.
Even if men be bad, why should they be rejected?
Therefore the sage is always a good saviour of men,

And no man is rejected;
He is a good saviour of things,
And nothing is rejected:
This is called double enlightenment.
Therefore good men are bad men's instructors,
And bad men are good men's materials.
Those who do not esteem their instructors,
And those who do not love their materials,
Though expedient, are in fact greatly confused.
This is essential subtlety.

TAO-TE-KING

CHRISTIANITY

DAY 335

For Whom the Bell Tolls

The church is catholic, universal, as are all her actions; all that she does belongs to all. When she baptizes a child, that action concerns me; for that child is thereby connected to that head which is my head too, and ingrafted into that body whereof I am a member. And when she buries a man, that action concerns me: all mankind is of one another, and is one volume. . . . No man is an island, entire of itself, every man is a piece of the continent, a part of the main. If a clod be washed away by the sea, Europe is the less, as well as if a manor of thy friend's or of thine own were; any man's death diminishes me, because I am involved in mankind; and therefore never send to know for whom the bell tolls; it tolls for thee. Neither can we call this a begging of misery, or a borrowing of misery, as though we were not miserable enough of ourselves, but must fetch in more from the next house, in taking upon us the misery of our neighbours. Truly it were an excusable covetousness if we did, for affliction is a treasure, and scarce any man has enough of it. No man hath affliction enough that is not matured and ripened by it, and made fit for God by that affliction. If a man carry treasure in bullion, or in a wedge of gold, and have none coined into current money, his treasure will not defray him as he travels. Tribulation is treasure in the nature of it, but it is not current money in the use of it, except as we get nearer and nearer our home, heaven, by it. Another man may be sick too, and sick to death, and this affliction may lie in his bowels, as gold in a mine, and be of no use to him; but this bell, that tells me of his affliction, digs out and applies that gold to me: if by this consideration of another's danger I take mine own into contemplation, and so secure my self, by making recourse to my God, who is our only security.

JOHN DONNE

DAY 336   HINDUISM
Self-Rule and Hospitality

A king must first subdue himself, and then
Vanquish his enemies. How can a prince
Who cannot rule himself enthral his foes?
To curb the senses is to conquer self.

Even to foes who visit us as guests
Due hospitality should be displayed;
The tree screens with its leaves the man who fells it.

MAHABHARATA

DAY 337   CHRISTIANITY
The Practice of Religion

It is essential to religion, to live according to the difference of good and evil: religion issues in holiness, uprightness, integrity, and separation from iniquity.

No man is born with wisdom and virtue; but every man hath himself as he useth himself.

Follow not blindfold, but as having one eye upon the rule, and the other upon the example.

BENJAMIN WHICHCOTE

211

Reflections on Age and Effort

The small hand of the child cannot reach the high shelf. The large hand of the adult cannot enter the narrow neck of the calabash.

The young palm branch tries to reach the sky. What offense did the old branch commit, that it did not succeed?

The river carries away an elderly person who does not know his weight.

The god who favors a lazy man does not exist. It is one's hands that bring prosperity.

When you help a lazy man, you ought to help him thoroughly. If you buy him a cloth, better have it dyed in indigo too.

Everybody who comes to this world, must become something. Only we don't know what.

However sharp the knife, it cannot scratch its own handle.

YORUBA PROVERBS

Romantic Love and Active Love

Never be afraid of your own cowardliness in attaining love, and do not be too much afraid of your bad actions, either. I'm sorry I cannot say anything more comforting to you, for, compared with romantic love, active love is something severe and terrifying. Romantic love yearns for an immediate act of heroism that can be achieved rapidly and that everyone can see. This sort of love really reaches a point where a man will even sacrifice his life provided his ordeal doesn't last long and is over quickly just as though it took place on a stage, and provided all are looking on and applauding. But active love means hard work and tenacity, and for some people it is, perhaps, a whole science. But I predict that at the very moment when you will realize with horror that, far from getting nearer to your goal, you are, in spite of all your efforts, actually further away from it than ever, I predict that at that very moment you will suddenly attain your goal and will behold clearly the miraculous power of the Lord who has all the time been loving and mysteriously guiding you.

FYODOR DOSTOEVSKY

DAY 340   SIKHISM
In the Sight of God

Instigated by their hearts, men lose patience and beg again and again to their ruin.

Covetousness is a black dungeon, demerits the fetters on the feet.

Wealth ever beateth the soul with its mallet, while sin sitteth as a judge.

Man shall be either good or bad, O Lord, as Thou lookest on him.

NANAK

DAY 341   CHRISTIANITY
Commitment to God

What we can *do* is a small thing; but we can will and aspire to great things. Thus, if a man cannot be great, he can yet be good in will; and what he, with his whole heart and mind, love and desire, wills to be, that without doubt he most truly is. It is little we can bring to pass; but our will and desire may be large. Nay, they may grow till they lose themselves in the infinite abyss of God. Not that we ought to think within ourselves that we wish to be this or that, like such a saint or angel, for we ought to be much more than we can conceive or fathom: wherefore our part is to give ourselves over to God and leave ourselves utterly in His hands, being wholly His. And if you cannot be as entirely His as you wish to be, be His as much as you may attain to; but whatever you are, be that truly and entirely; and what you cannot be, that be contented not to be in a sincere spirit of resignation, for God's sake and in Him. So shall you peradventure possess more of

213

God in lacking than in having. Therefore be God's; yield to His hand, let Him do in you, and to you, and with you, what He will; and then nothing here or hereafter shall be able to confound you.

JOHANNES TAULER

DAY 342   ANTI-CONFUCIANISM
Heaven Loves the People

How do we know Heaven loves the people? Because it teaches them all. How do we know it teaches them all? Because it claims them all. How do we know it claims them all? Because it accepts sacrifices from them all. How do we know it accepts sacrifices from all? Because within the four seas all who live on grains feed oxen and sheep with grass, and dogs and pigs with grains, and prepare clean cakes and wine to do sacrifices to God on High and the spirits. Claiming all the people, why will Heaven not love them? Moreover, as I have said, for the murder of one innocent individual there will be one calamity. Who is it that murders the innocent? It is man. Who is it that sends down the calamity? It is Heaven. If Heaven should be thought of as not loving the people, why should it send down calamities for the murder of man by man? So, I know Heaven loves the people.

MOTSE

DAY 343   HINDUISM
Immortality a Present Possession

True joy is not Beyond,
In some luxurious paradise,
In total loss of self within the absolute: 4

True joy is here,
With Him:

Seize on that joy, with eager haste, my soul,
Here in this world, have all thy need fulfilled,
In Him, by Him!

Pray not for utter merging,
Pray not for paradise,
Know God, take God, love God,
Now.

TUKARAM

DAY 344 JUDAISM

Equality

A man came to Raba and said, "The prefect of my town has ordered me to kill so and so, or he will kill me." Raba replied, "Let him kill you; do you commit no murder. Why should you think that your blood is redder than his? Perhaps his is redder than yours."

PESACHIM

DAY 345 HINDUISM

The Greatest Virtues

Truthfulness, mercy, purification, forgiveness,
Discrimination between propriety and impropriety,
Control over the mind, subjugation of the senses,
Harmlessness, charity, simplicity, contentment,

Total refrainment from vile deeds, introspection,
Inspection of the fruitless actions of men,
An equitable distribution of eatables and other things,
Identification of other men with one's own self,

Remembrance of Him Who is the refuge of the illustrious ones,
Service unto Him, His adoration,
Offering of salutations unto Him, friendship towards Him,
And dedication of one's own self unto Him—

These have been asserted to be the greatest of virtues,
The common property of all human beings.
The religion that beareth all these features
Can afford solace unto every soul.

BHAGAVATA PURANA

215

DAY 346   BABYLONIAN RELIGION
The Fear of God

In thy learning look at the tablet:
Fear of God brings forth grace;
Sacrifice gives increase of life;
And prayer cancels sin.
He who fears the gods will not call in vain.

ACADIAN COUNSELS OF WISDOM
AKKADIAN COUNSELS OF WISDOM

DAY 347   JUDAISM
Sayings of the Baal Shem

What does it mean, when people say that Truth goes over all
the world? It means that Truth is driven out of one place after
another, and must wander on and on.

Alas! the world is full of enormous lights and mysteries, and
man shuts them from himself with one small hand!

When I weld my spirit to God, I let my mouth say what it will,
for then all my words are bound to their root in Heaven.

RABBI ISRAEL BEN ELIEZER

DAY 348   CHRISTIANITY
Aphorisms

Nothing is more reasonable than that we should be that to one
another, which God is to us all.

Those who are evil themselves are hard to believe the good that
is spoken of others.

We are made one for another, and each is a supply to his
neighbor.

No man is wise enough for his own direction, powerful enough
for his own defense, or good enough for his own satisfaction.

BENJAMIN WHICHCOTE

216

Absorption Leads to Salvation

Quickly I come
To those who offer me
Every action,
Worship me only,
Their dearest delight,
With devotion undaunted.

Because they love me
These are my bondsmen
And I shall save them
From mortal sorrow
And all the waves
Of Life's deathly ocean.

Be absorbed in me,
Lodge your mind in me:
Thus you shall dwell in me,
Do not doubt it,
Here and hereafter.

If you cannot become absorbed in me, then try to reach me
by repeated concentration. If you lack the strength to concentrate,
then devote yourself to works which will please me. For, by
working for my sake only, you will achieve perfection. If you
cannot even do this, then surrender yourself to me altogether.
Control the lusts of your heart, and renounce the fruits of every
action.

BHAGAVAD-GITA

Nearness to God

Someone asked Rabyah, "Walking over water, flying in the
air—are not these proofs of attaining nearness to God?"

Rabyah replied, "No, never. Even the smallest fish can move about in the water as it likes and the tiniest fly can move about in the air with perfect ease. These are trifling things. They do not testify to the realization of spiritual reflection—they are external things, they have no relation to spiritual life."

TAPASI RABYAH

DAY 351 SIKHISM

Man's Best Aspiration

Some saints are genuine and some impostors,
Some receive their honor at the threshold,
Some saints shine at the gateway of the ruler,
And some think sincerely of the Guru.

Though thought and speech be far extended,
This measures not the works of the creator,
Not by the bull but by the law of mercy
Joy becomes man's guardian and guidance.

Who comprehendeth this hath truth discovered,
Nor rests his burden faithless on the bull,
There are so many earths, another and another,
A burden far beyond his power to uphold it.

Creatures, castes, of many shades of color,
Have ever been described in varied phrase,
Many who have known the art of writing
Have written many essays on such themes.

Impressive are the varied forms of beauty,
Who knows the generous bounty of the whole?
How many issues out of one source flowing—
A hundred thousand rivers from one spring.

What mighty power for man to fix his thought on!
No self-denial comprehends it all,
To please thee is a man's best aspiration,
O thou who art eternal, ever dwelling in repose.

THE JAPJI

Pay Thy Debts

From poison you may take the food of life,
The purest gold from lumps of impure earth,
Examples of good conduct from a foe,
Sweet speech and gentleness from a child,
Something from all; from men of low degree
Lessons of wisdom, if you are humble.

LAW OF MANU

He Who Is of God Hears the Words of God

Dear children, you should not stop hearing or telling the word of God because you do not always live by it or keep it in mind. For if you love it and crave it, it will surely be given to you, and you will enjoy it forever with God, according to the measure of your craving. Some people speak of high things which they do not understand, and, seeing that they have no share in them, turn away with aversion. They do not even like to hear about them, and do not want others to think about them and seek them. Yes, they hear of high things and say: "That is not my way of thinking; I had better not try to put it into practice, for I would not keep it and then I would be right where I was in the first place." So they turn away from the truth, and turn others away, too, as if it did not concern them at all, and they settle contentedly in their own ways, though they know in the bottom of their hearts that their ways are not the best that they might be. This is an infallible token that these people will never reach the highest point they are capable of reaching, nor will they partake of the highest, pure absolute goodness, unless they undergo a painful struggle for it.

JOHANNES TAULER

219

Bear with Patience

Bear railing words with patience, never meet
An angry man with anger, nor return
Reviling for reviling, smite not him
Who smites thee, let thy speech and acts be gentle.

MAHABHARATA

Hope in the Lord

Out of the depths have I cried unto thee, O Lord.

Lord, hear my voice: let thine ears be attentive to the voice of my supplications.

If thou, Lord, shouldest mark iniquities, O Lord, who shall stand?

But there is forgiveness with thee, that thou mayest be feared.

I wait for the Lord, my soul doth wait, and in his word do I hope.

My soul waiteth for the Lord more than they that watch for the morning: I say, more than they that watch for the morning.

Let Israel hope in the Lord: for with the Lord there is mercy, and with him is plenteous redemption.

And he shall redeem Israel from all his iniquities.

PSALM 130

Where the Earth Feels Most Happy

O Maker of the material world, thou Holy One! Which is the first place where the Earth feels most happy?

Ahura Mazda answered: "It is the place whereon one of the

faithful steps forward, O Spitama Zarathustra! with the log in his hand, the Baresma in his hand, the milk in his hand, the mortar in his hand, lifting up his voice in good accord with religion and beseeching Mithra, the lord of the rolling country-side, and Rama Hvastra."

O Maker of the material world, thou Holy One! Which is the second place where the Earth feels most happy?

Ahura Mazda answered: "It is the place whereon one of the faithful erects a house with a priest within, with cattle, with a wife, with children, and good herds within; and wherein afterwards the cattle continue to thrive, virtue to thrive, fodder to thrive, the dog to thrive, the wife to thrive, the child to thrive, the fire to thrive, and every blessing of life to thrive."

O Maker of the material world, thou Holy One! Which is the third place where the Earth feels most happy?

Ahura Mazda answered: "It is the place where one of the faithful sows most corn, grass, and fruit, O Spitama Zarathustra! Where he waters ground that is dry, or drains ground that is too wet."

O Maker of the material world, thou Holy One! Which is the fourth place where the Earth feels most happy?

Ahura Mazda answered: "It is the place where there is most increase of flocks and herds!"

VENDIDAD

DAY 357   HINDUISM

Man's Extremity

Ah, then, O God, the efforts all are vain
By which I've sought thy blessed feet to gain.
    First there was loving faith, but faith I've none;
Nowise my restless soul can I restrain.

Then pious deeds, but no good will have I
For these; nor wealth to help the poor thereby;
    I know not how to honour Brahman guests;
Alas! the springs of love in me are dry.

221

I cannot serve the guru or the saint;
Not mine to chant the name, with toil to faint,
  Perform the sacred rites, renounce the world.
I cannot hold my senses in restraint.

My heart has never trod the pilgrim's way;
The vows I make I know not how to pay.
  "Ah, God is here," I cry. Not so, not so.
For me distinctions have not passed away.

Therefore, I come, O God, to plead for grace,
I, worthy only of a servant's place.
  No store of merit such an one requires.
My firm resolve is taken, Tuka says.

TUKARAM

DAY 358   ISLAM
Immediate Knowledge

Come, recognize that your sensation and imagination and under-
  standing are like the reed-cane on which children ride.
The spiritual man's knowledge bears him aloft; the sensual man's
  knowledge is a burden.
God hath said, *Like an ass laden with books:* heavy is the knowl-
  edge that is not inspired by Him;
But if you carry it for no selfish ends, the load will be lifted
  and you will feel delight.
How can you become free without the wine of Him,
  O you who are content with the sign of Him?
From attribute and name what is born? Phantasy; but phantasy
  shows the way to the Truth.
Do you know any name without a reality? Or, have you ever
  plucked a rose from R.O.S.E.?
You have pronounced the name: go, seek the thing named. The
  moon is in the sky, not in the water.
Would you rise beyond name and letter, make yourself entirely
  pure,

222

And behold in your own heart all the knowledge of the prophets,
without book, without learning, without preceptor.

JALALU'L-DIN RUMI

DAY 359   SIKHISM
Truth and Falsehood

Truth and falsehood stand to one another
    In the relation of a stone to an earthen vessel.
If a stone be thrown at an earthen vessel,
    It is the earthen vessel which will break.

If the earthen vessel be thrown at a stone,
    It is again the earthen vessel which will break.
In either case
    It is the earthen vessel that suffers.

Truth is immovable and on safe ground.
    Falsehood stands, and trembles, on an insecure basis.
Falsehood, which is deceitful, ever ails,
    Truth is ever safe and whole.

BHAI GUR DAS

DAY 360   HINDUISM
The Narrow Gate

Heaven's gate is very narrow and minute,
It cannot be perceived by foolish men,
Blinded by vain illusions of the world.
Even the clear-sighted who discern the way,
And seek to enter, find the portal barred
And hard to be unlocked. Its massive bolts
Are pride and passion, avarice and lust.

MAHABHARATA

The Deathless Fruit

Faith is the seed, austerity the rain,
    Wisdom my yoke and plough;
My pole is modesty, mind is the strap,
    And I have mindfulness
For share and goad. Warded in act and word,
    In eating temperate,
With truth I clear the weeds; and full of bliss
    Is my deliverance.
To a security from moil doth draw
    Vigour, my team in yoke:
And on it goes, nor turns it back; it goes
    Where is no suffering.
And thuswise is this ploughing ploughed, and thence
    There comes the deathless fruit;
And whoso hath this ploughing ploughed, set free
    Is he from every ill.

                                    SUTTA NIPATA

Man's Becoming Real

It is the characteristic of Heaven to *be* the Real. It is the characteristic of man to be coming-to-be-real. (For a man) to be real [i.e., to have achieved realness] is to hit the Mean without effort, to have it without thinking of it, entirely to be centered in the Way: (in other words) to be a sage.

To be coming-to-be-real is to choose the good and to hold fast to it. This involves learning about the good, asking about it, thinking it over carefully, getting it clear by contrast, and faithfully putting it into practice. If there is any part about which he has not learnt or asked questions, which he has not thought over and got clear by contrast, or which he has not put into practice, he sets to work to learn and ask and think and get clear and put into practice. If he does not get the required result, he still does not give up working. When he sees other men succeeding by one effort, or it may be a hundred, he is prepared to add a hundredfold to his own efforts. The man who can last this course, although he is stupid, will come to understand; although he is weak, will become strong.

TZU SSU

DAY 363 JUDAISM

An Overpowering Welcome

When Rabbi Phineas Hurwitz came to Frankfurt to take up the post of Rabbi, he received an overpowering welcome. Thousands of people surrounded his carriage. A friend asked how he felt in this hour of triumph. The Rabbi replied: "I imagined that I was a corpse, being borne to the cemetery in the company of multitudes attending the funeral."

HASIDIC STORY

DAY 364 HINDUISM

"He Shall Not Perish"

My face is equal
To all creation,
Loving no one
Nor hating any.

Nevertheless,
My devotees dwell
Within me always:
I also show forth
And am seen within them.

Though a man be soiled
With the sins of a lifetime,
Let him but love me,
Rightly resolved,
In utter devotion:

I see no sinner,
That man is holy.
Holiness soon
Shall refashion his nature
To peace eternal;
O son of Kunti,
Of this be certain:
The man that loves me,
He shall not perish.

BHAGAVAD-GITA

DAY 365   TAOISM

The Folly of Excess

A man on tiptoe cannot stand firm;
A man astride cannot walk on;
A man who displays himself cannot shine;
A man who approves himself cannot be noted;
A man who praises himself cannot have merit;
A man who glories in himself cannot excel;
These, when compared with Tao, are called:
    "Excess in food and overdoing in action."
Even in other things, mostly, they are rejected;
Therefore the man of Tao does not stay with them.

TAO-TE-KING

Sources and Bibliography

DAY 1 Archbishop Fénelon, *Golden Thoughts*. New York and Boston: H. M. Caldwell, 1901, pp. 130-131.

2 Edward Conze, ed., *Buddhist Texts Through the Ages*. Oxford: Bruno Cassirer, Ltd., 1954, p. 274.

3 Adapted from Monier Williams, ed., *Indian Wisdom*. London: W. H. Allen, 1875, pp. 446-447.

4 James Legge, ed., *The Chinese Classics*. New York: John W. Lovell Co., 1870, Part I, pp. 18, 25-26, 30.

5 Arthur J. Arberry, trans., *The Koran Interpreted*. London: G. Allen & Unwin, Ltd., and New York: The Macmillan Co., 1955, Vol. II, p. 339.

6 Herbert A. Giles, trans., *Chuang Tzu, Mystic, Moralist and Social Reformer*. London: Bernard Quaritch Ltd., 1889, p. 253.

7 Psalm 19, King James Version.

8 Søren Kierkegaard, *Works of Love* (translated by D. F. Swenson and L. M. Swenson). Princeton: Princeton University Press, 1949, pp. 56-57.

9 Adapted from Monier Williams, ed., *Indian Wisdom* (see Day 3), p. 150.

10 Louis I. Newman and Samuel Spitz, eds., *The Hasidic Anthology*. New York: Bloch Publishing Co., 1944, p. 205.

11 Edward Conze, ed., *Buddhist Texts Through the Ages* (see Day 2), p. 278.

12 James Legge, ed., *The Chinese Classics* (see Day 4), Part I, pp. 80, 82.

13 C. E. Wilson, trans., *The Masnavi*. London: Probsthain & Co., 1910, pp. 472-473.

14 *The Apocrypha, An American Translation*, by Edgar J. Goodspeed. Chicago: The University of Chicago Press, 1939, p. 78.

15 The Homilies of St. Chrysostom: On Collos. 10, in *Selections From the Writings of St. Chrysostom*, Church Lamps, Seeley, 1882.

16 Adapted from Monier Williams, ed., *Indian Wisdom* (see Day 3), pp. 517-518.

17 F. Max Müller, ed., *The Sacred Books of the East*. Oxford: Clarendon Press, 1881, Vol. X, Part I, pp. 61-62.

18 Adapted from James Legge, trans., *The Sacred Books of the East*. Oxford: Clarendon Press, 1885, Vol. 28, pp. 236-238.

19 F. Max Müller, ed., *The Sacred Books of the East* (see Day 17), Vol. X, Part I, pp. 61-62.

20 Arthur J. Arberry, trans., *The Koran Interpreted* (see Day 5), Vol. II, p. 356.

21 Louis I. Newman and Samuel Spitz, eds., *The Hasidic Anthology* (see Day 10), p. 116.

22 Herbert A. Giles, trans., *Chuang Tzu, Mystic, Moralist and Social Reformer* (see Day 6), pp. 223-224.

23 James B. Pritchard, ed., *Ancient Near Eastern Texts Relating to the Old Testament*, translated by John A. Wilson. Princeton: Princeton University Press, 1950, pp. 422-424, *passim*.

24 Adapted from *Theologia Germanica*, edited by Dr. Franz Pfeiffer, translated by Susanna Winkworth. New York: Macmillan, 1901, pp. 192-194.

25 F. Max Müller, trans., *The Sacred Books of the East*. Oxford: Clarendon Press, 1898, Vol. X, pp. 45-46.

26 Adapted from Maurice H.

Harris, *Hebraic Literature*. New York: Tudor Publishing Co., 1901, p. 313.

27 James Legge, ed., *The Chinese Classics* (see Day 4), Part II, pp. 158, 162.

28 Psalm 8, Revised Standard Version.

29 Monier Williams, ed., *The Wisdom of India*. London: W. H. Allen, 1895, p. 445.

30 Herbert A. Giles, trans., *Chuang Tzu, Mystic, Moralist and Social Reformer* (see Day 6), pp. 33-35.

31 Sir Jogendra S. Singh, ed., *The Invocation of Sheikh Abdullah Ansari of Herat*. London: Murray, 1939, pp. 32, 54.

32 Archbishop Fénelon, *Golden Thoughts* (see Day 1), pp. 108-110.

33 Arthur Waley, *Three Ways of Thought in Ancient China*. New York: Doubleday, 1956, pp. 78-79.

34 Adapted from Irving Fineman, *Hear, Ye Sons*. New York: David McKay Company, Inc., 1933, pp. 238-239.

35 W. Montgomery Watt, ed., *The Faith and Practice of Al-Ghazali*. London: G. Allen & Unwin, Ltd., and New York: Macmillan, 1953, p. 134.

36 Ralph T. H. Griffith, ed., *The Hymns of the Rigveda*. Benares: E. J. Lazarus, 1897, 2nd ed., Vol. II, pp. 575-576.

37 Adapted from F. Max Müller, ed., *The Sacred Books of the East* (see Day 25), Vol. X, pp. 34-35.

38 Ecclesiastes 12:1-8, King James Version.

39 William Law, *A Serious Call to a Devout and Holy Life*. New York: E. P. Dutton, Everyman Edition, 1906, pp. 162-163.

40 W. Montgomery Watt, ed., *The Faith and Practice of Al-Ghazali* (see Day 35), p. 133.

41 Ch'u Ta-Kao, trans., *Tao-Te-Ching*. London: The Buddhist Lodge, 1937, Ch. LXVII.

42 Martin Buber, *Hasidism and Modern Man*. New York: Horizon Press, 1958, pp. 194-195.

43 Edward Conze, ed., *Buddhist Texts Through the Ages* (see Day 2), pp. 71-72.

44 Isaiah 5:20-24, Revised Standard Version.

45 *The Sayings of Sri Ramakrishna*, compiled by Swami Abhedananda. New York: the Vedanta Society, 1903, pp. 141, 142, 144-145.

46 James Legge, ed., *The Chinese Classics* (see Day 4), Part II, pp. 112-114.

47 Matthew 5:1-16, King James Version.

48 Adapted from Maurice H. Harris, ed., *Hebraic Literature* (see Day 26), p. 94.

49 Adapted from Herbert A. Giles, trans., *Chuang Tzu, Mystic, Moralist and Social Reformer* (see Day 6), p. 236.

50 R. A. Nicholson, ed., *Rumi: Poet and Mystic*. London: G. Allen & Unwin, Ltd., and New York: The Macmillan Company, 1950, p. 64.

51 Adapted from James Legge, ed., *The Chinese Classics* (see Day 4), Part II, pp. 150-151.

52 Proverbs 23:29-35, Revised Standard Version.

53 F. Max Müller, ed., *The Sacred Books of the East* (see Day 17), Vol. X, Part I, pp. 64-66.

54 Adapted from Monier Williams, ed., *Indian Wisdom* (see Day 3), pp. 447-448.

55 Reinhold Niebuhr, *The Nature and Destiny of Man*. New York: Charles Scribner's Sons, 1943, Vol. II, p. 1.

56 Nikolai Berdyaev, *The Destiny of Man*. New York: Harper & Row (Torchbook), and London: Geoffrey Bles, Ltd., 1955, pp. 121-122.

57 C. E. Wilson, trans., *The Masnavi* (see Day 13).

58 Adapted from James Legge, ed., *The Chinese Classics*. London: Trubner, 1861, Vol. I, pp. 230-231.

59 F. Max Müller, ed., *The Sa-*

cred *Books of the East* (see Day 17), Vol. X, Part I, pp. 77-78.

60 Adapted from Maurice H. Harris, ed., *Hebraic Literature* (see Day 26), p. 166.

61 Herbert A. Giles, trans., *Chuang Tzu, Mystic, Moralist and Social Reformer* (see Day 6), pp. 30, 32.

62 Herman Jacobi, trans. Jaina Sutras, *The Sacred Books of the East*. Oxford: Clarendon Press, 1895, Vol. 45, pp. 18, 19, 34, 40, 63, 67.

63 C. W. Eliot, ed., *Harvard Classics*. New York: P. F. Collier & Son Co., 1909, Vol. VII, p. 272.

64 Adapted from James Legge, trans., *The Sacred Books of the East* (see Day 18), Vol. 27, pp. 378-379.

65 Adapted from Maurice H. Harris, *Hebraic Literature* (see Day 26), p. 291.

66 Herbert A. Giles, trans., *Chuang Tzu, Mystic, Moralist and Social Reformer* (see Day 6), p. 20.

67 Adopted from W. H. D. Rouse, trans., *The Jataka*, Vol. II, E. B. Cowell, ed. Cambridge University Press, 1895, Book II, Story 185, pp. 68-69.

68 Ecclesiastes 5:8-15, Revised Standard Version.

69 *The Sayings of Sri Ramakrishna*, compiled by Swami Abhedananda (see Day 45), p. 210.

70 Adapted from C. E. Wilson, trans., *The Masnavi* (see Day 13).

71 Jacques Maritain, *Ransoming the Time*. New York: Charles Scribner's Sons, 1948, pp. 139-140.

72 Maurice H. Harris, ed., *Hebraic Literature* (see Day 26), p. 124.

73 Herbert A. Giles, trans., *Chuang Tzu, Mystic, Moralist and Social Reformer* (see Day 6), pp. 52-53.

74 T. W. and C. A. F. Rhys Davids, trans., "Dialogues of the Buddha," Part III, in the *Sacred Books of the Buddhists*, Vol. IV. London: Oxford University Press, 1921.

75 *The Sayings of Sri Ramakrishna*, compiled by Swami Abhedananda (see Day 45), pp. 177-178.

76 Arthur J. Arberry, trans., *The Koran Interpreted* (see Day 5), Vol. 1, pp. 241-242.

77 Isaiah 35:5-10, King James Version.

78 James Legge, ed., *The Chinese Classics* (see Day 4), Part II, pp. 153-154.

79 Whitney J. Oates, ed., *The Stoic and Epicurean Philosophers*. New York: Random House, 1940, p. 497.

80 John Calvin, *Institutes of the Christian Religion*, trans. John Allen, 1813. Philadelphia: Presbyterian Board of Christian Education, 6th American edition, 1935, Vol. 1, pp. 649-650.

81 W. Montgomery Watt, ed., *The Faith and Practice of Al-Ghazali* (see Day 35), p. 137.

82 Herbert A. Giles, trans., *Chuang Tzu, Mystic, Moralist and Social Reformer* (see Day 6), pp. 258-259.

83 Edmond Fleg, ed., *The Jewish Anthology*. New York: Harcourt, Brace & World, 1925, p. 120.

84 Monier Williams, trans., *Sakuntala*. London: W. H. Allen, 1853, p. 129.

85 S. G. Champion, *The Eleven Religions*. New York: E. P. Dutton, 1945, p. 100.

86 Nāgarjuna (LuTrub), *The Tree of Wisdom*, trans. by W. L. Campbell from the Tibetan version (She-Rab Dong-Bu) of the Sanskrit original (Prajna Danda). Calcutta: Calcutta University at the Baptist Mission Press, 1919, pp. 12, 76, 108.

87 S. G. Champoin, *The Eleven Religions* (see Day 85), p. 100.

88 Adapted from M. A. Macauliffe, *The Sikh Religion*. Oxford: Clarendon Press, 1909, Vol. 3, pp. 18-19.

229

89 Matthew 5:38-48, King James Version.

90 Herbert A. Giles, trans., *Chuang Tzu, Mystic, Moralist and Social Reformer* (see Day 6), p. 27.

91 *The Sayings of Sri Ramakrishna*, compiled by Swami Abhedananda (see Day 45), pp. 145-147.

92 Joseph H. Hertz, ed., *A Book of Jewish Thoughts*. New York: Bloch Publishing Co., 1926, p. 290.

93 R. A. Nicholson, ed., *Rumi: Poet and Mystic* (see Day 50), p. 76.

94 Jeremiah 7:3-9, 17-20, King James Version.

95 Ivan Chen, trans., *The Book of Filial Duty*. New York: E. P. Dutton, 1920, pp. 28-29.

96 Monier Williams, ed., *Indian Wisdom* (see Day 3), p. 444.

97 Clark Wissler and D. C. Duvall, "Mythology of Blackfoot Indians," *Papers of the American Museum of Natural History*, New York, September 1908, Vol. II, Part I, p. 21.

98 Reinhold Niebuhr, "A Faith for History's Greatest Crisis," *Fortune*, July 1942, p. 131.

99 Arthur J. Arberry, *The Koran Interpreted* (see Day 5), pp. 50-51.

100 Herbert A. Giles, trans., *Chuang Tzu, Mystic, Moralist and Social Reformer* (see Day 6), pp. 36-37.

101 Psalm 27, King James Version.

102 Shao Chang Lee, ed., *Popular Buddhism in China*. Shanghai: Commercial Press, Ltd., 1939, pp. 21-22.

103 Lin Yutang, ed., *The Wisdom of Confucius*. New York: Random House, 1938, p. 181.

104 Adapted from Maurice H. Harris, ed., *Hebraic Literature* (see Day 26), p. 326.

105 Monier Williams, ed., *Indian Wisdom* (see Day 3), pp. 461-462.

106 Adapted from *Theologia Germanica* (see Day 24), pp. 133-136.

107 Mrs. Rhys Davids, trans., *The Book of the Kindred Sayings* (Samyutta-Nikaya). London: Oxford University Press, 1917, Part I, p. 110.

108 Monier Williams, ed., *Indian Wisdom* (see Day 3), p. 462.

109 Søren Kierkegaard, *Works of Love* (see Day 8), pp. 307-308.

110 James Legge, ed., *The Chinese Classics* (see Day 4), pp. 42, 48-49.

111 Maurice H. Harris, ed., *Hebraic Literature* (see Day 26), pp. 296-297.

112 Arthur J. Arberry, trans., *The Koran Interpreted* (see Day 5), Vol. I, pp. 305-306.

113 Lionel Giles, trans., *Taoist Teachings from the Book of Lieh Tzu*. London: John Murray, New York: E. P. Dutton & Co., Inc., 1912, 2nd ed., 1947, pp. 119-120.

114 John Clark Archer, *The Sikhs*. Princeton: Princeton University Press, 1946, p. 126-127.

115 Newly translated for this edition by J. S. Winkler and E. O. Wruck from Angelus Silesius (Johannes Scheffler), *Cherubinischer Wandersmann*. Sulzbach: J. E. von Seidel Verlag, 1829.

116 E. M. Hare, trans., *Woven Cadences of Early Buddhists*. London: Oxford University Press, 1945, pp. 96-97.

117 Paraphrase by William Robert Miller for this edition, based on C. E. Wilson, trans., *The Masnavi*. London: Probsthain & Co., 1910.

118 *The Apocrypha, An American Translation* by Edgar J. Goodspeed (see Day 14), p. 179.

119 Herbert A. Giles, trans., *Chuang Tzu, Mystic Moralist and Social Reformer* (see Day 6), p. 68.

120 Maurice H. Harris, ed., *Hebraic Literature* (see Day 26), p. 315.

121 James Legge, ed., *The Chinese Classics* (see Day 4), Part I, pp. 126-127.

230

122 Ecclesiastes 11:1-8. Standard American Edition of the Revised Version of the Bible, New York: Thomas Nelson & Sons, 1901.

123 Adapted from Monier Williams, *Indian Wisdom* (see Day 3), p. 441.

124 Thomas Fuller, *Good Thoughts in Bad Times*. New York: E. P. Dutton, 1876, pp. 20-21.

125 Arthur J. Arberry, *The Koran Interpreted* (see Day 5), Vol. II, p. 231.

126 Jeremiah 17:5-9, King James Version.

127 K. J. Saunders, ed., *The Heart of Buddhism*. Oxford: Clarendon Press, 1915, pp. 73-75.

128 Herbert A. Giles, trans., *Chuang Tzu, Mystic, Moralist and Social Reformer* (see Day 6), p. 244.

129 Maurice H. Harris, ed., *Hebraic Literature* (see Day 26), p. 176.

130 *Passages from the Life and Writings of George Fox*, taken from his Journal. Philadelphia: Friends' Book Store, 1880, pp. 36-37.

131 Herbert A. Giles, trans., *Chuang Tzu, Mystic, Moralist and Social Reformer* (see Day 6), p. 217.

132 Maurice M. Harris, ed., *Hebraic Literature* (see Day 26), pp. 254-255.

133 Monier Williams, ed., *Indian Wisdom* (see Day 3), p. 445.

134 Arthur J. Arberry, trans., *The Koran Interpreted* (see Day 5), Vol. II, p. 329.

135 Epiphanius Wilson, ed., *Chinese Literature* (The World's Classics), London and New York: Colonial Press, 1900, pp. 20-21.

136 E. Conze, ed., *Buddhist Texts Through the Ages* (see Day 2), p. 55.

137 *The Apocrypha, An American Translation*, by Edgar J. Goodspeed (see Day 14), pp. 101-102.

138 James Legge, ed., *The Chinese Classics* (see Day 4), Vol. IV, Part II, pp. 250-253.

139 Matthew 6:19-24, King James Version.

140 Herbert A. Giles, trans., *Chuang Tzu, Mystic, Moralist and Social Reformer* (see Day 6), pp. 218-219.

141 Howard Thurman, *Deep River*. New York: Harper & Row, 1945, pp. 75-76.

142 E. Conze, ed., *Buddhist Texts Through the Ages* (see Day 2), p. 34.

143 James Legge, ed., *The Chinese Classics* (see Day 58), p. 350.

144 C. G. Montefiore and H. Loewe, eds., *A Rabbinic Anthology*. London: Macmillan & Co., Ltd., 1938, p. 178.

145 Arthur J. Arberry, trans., *The Koran Interpreted* (see Day 5), Vol. II, pp. 35-36.

146 Micah 4:2-7, King James Version.

147 Monier Williams, ed., *Indian Wisdom* (see Day 3), pp. 459-461.

148 Proverbs 9:7-9, Standard American Edition of the Revised Version of the Bible (see Day 122).

149 Adapted from R. H. Charles, *The Testament of the Twelve Patriarchs*. London: Society for Promoting Christian Knowledge, 1917, pp. 85-86.

150 E. Conze, ed., *Buddhist Texts Through the Ages* (see Day 2), pp. 87-88.

151 *The Apocrypha, An American Translation*, by Edgar J. Goodspeed (see Day 14), pp. 247-248.

152 Herbert A. Giles, trans., *Chuang Tzu, Mystic, Moralist and Social Reformer* (see Day 6), pp. 430-431.

153 Arthur J. Arberry, trans., *The Koran Interpreted* (see Day 5), Vol. II, pp. 101-102.

154 Søren Kierkegaard, *Concluding Unscientific Postscript*, trans. by D. F. Swenson and W. Lowrie, Princeton: Princeton University Press, 1944, p. 521.

155 F. Max Müller, ed., *The Sacred Books of the East*. Oxford: Clarendon Press, 1900, Vol. XV, pp. 175-179.

156 Whitney J. Oates, ed., *The Stoic and Epicurean Philosophers* (see Day 79), pp. 572-573.

157 Archbishop Fénelon, *Golden Thoughts* (see Day 1), pp. 81-82.

158 F. Max Müller, ed., *The Sacred Books of the East*. Oxford: Clarendon Press, 1885, Vol. XXVIII, p. 93.

159 Savonarola, *The Triumph of the Cross* quoted in the anthology *Valiant for the Truth*, edited by David Otis Fuller, New York: McGraw-Hill, 1961, pp. 106 ff.

160 Monier Williams, ed., *Indian Wisdom* (see Day 3), p. 444.

161 S. Beal, ed., *Texts from the Buddhist Canon*. London: Routledge, 1878, pp. 148-149.

162 Proverbs 6:6-11, Standard American Edition of the Revised Standard Version of the Bible (see Day 122).

163 Lewis Browne, ed., *The World's Great Scriptures*. New York: Macmillan, 1946, p. 446.

164 Herbert A. Giles, trans., *Chuang Tzu, Mystic, Moralist and Social Reformer* (see Day 6), p. 82.

165 Baron Friedrich von Hügel, *Essays and Addresses on the Philosophy of Religion*, Second Series. London: J. M. Dent & Sons, Ltd., 1921, pp. 240-241.

166 Arthur J. Arberry, trans., *The Koran Interpreted* (see Day 5), Vol. II, p. 353.

167 *The Apocrypha, An American Translation*, by Edgar J. Goodspeed (see Day 14), pp. 260-261.

168 S. Beal, ed., *Texts from the Buddhist Canon* (see Day 161), pp. 119-120.

169 Monier Williams, ed., *Indian Wisdom* (see Day 3), p. 442.

170 Monier Williams, ed., *Indian Wisdom* (see Day 3), pp. 517-518.

171 Adapted from James Legge, ed., *The Chinese Classics* (see Day 58), Vol. I, pp. 272, 277.

172 C. G. Montefiore and H. Loewe, eds., *A Rabbinic Anthology* (see Day 144), p. 2.

173 Herbert A. Giles, trans., *Chuang Tzu, Mystic, Moralist and Social Reformer* (see Day 6), pp. 434-435.

174 Benjamin Jowett, trans., *The Dialogues of Plato*. New York: Random House, 1937, Vol. II, p. 487.

175 Matthew 16:24-28, King James Version.

176 Herbert A. Giles, trans., *Chuang Tzu, Mystic, Moralist and Social Reformer* (see Day 6), pp. 240-241.

177 Monier Williams, ed., *Indian Wisdom* (see Day 3), pp. 46-47.

178 Psalm 15, King James Version.

179 W. H. D. Rouse, trans., *The Jataka* (see Day 67), Vol. II, Book III, Story 300, p. 307.

180 W. A. Oldfather, trans., *Epictetus—The Discourses as Reported by Arrian, the Manual and Fragments*. Cambridge: Harvard University Press, Loeb Classical Library, 1928, Vol. II, pp. 511-515.

181 Richard Bell, trans., *Qur'an*. Edinburgh: T. and T. Clark, 1937, Surah 96.

182 Quoted from Kierkegaard's *Journal* in Walter Lowrie, *Kierkegaard*. Oxford: Oxford University Press, 1938, p. 588.

183 James Legge, ed., *The Chinese Classics* (see Day 4), Part I, p. 129.

184 A. Cohen, ed., *Everyman's Talmud*. London: J. M. Dent & Sons, Ltd., 1932, p. 92.

185 Matthew 21:27-32, King James Version.

186 Lewis Browne, ed., *The World's Great Scriptures* (see Day 163), pp. 446-447.

187 Monier Williams, ed., *Indian Wisdom* (see Day 3), p. 445.

188 Adapted from Madison C. Peters, ed., *Wit and Wisdom of the Talmud*. New York: Baker & Taylor, 1900, pp. 40-41.

189 Raïssa Maritain, ed., *Léon Bloy, Pilgrim of the Absolute*, trans. by John Coleman and Harry Lorin Binssé. New York: Pantheon Books, 1947, p. 219.

190 Herbert A. Giles, trans., *Chuang Tzu, Mystic, Moralist and Social Reformer* (see Day 6), pp. 184-185.

191 Winkler and Wruck, trans., Angelus Silesius, *Cherubinischer Wandersmann* (see Day 115).

192 James Legge, ed., *The Chinese Classics* (see Day 4), Part II, pp. 106-107.

193 *The Apocrypha, An American Translation*, by E. J. Goodspeed (see Day 14), pp. 239-240.

194 C. G. Montefiore and H. Loewe, eds., *A Rabbinic Anthology* (see Day 144), p. 166.

195 Matthew 22:15-22, King James Version.

196 Monier Williams, ed., *Indian Wisdom* (see Day 3), Law of Manu XI, p. 231.

197 Psalm 23, King James Version.

198 Y. P. Mei, trans., *The Works of Motse*. London: Probsthain, 1934, pp. 101-103.

199 Ch'u Ta-Kao, trans., *Tao-Te-Ching* (see Day 41), Ch. LXIII.

200 Arthur J. Arberry, trans., *The Koran Interpreted* (see Day 5), Vol. II, p. 341.

201 Adapted from Monier Williams, ed., *Indian Wisdom* (see Day 3), pp. 447-448.

202 Matthew 25:1-13, King James Version.

203 Ch'u Ta-Kao, trans., *Tao-Te-Ching* (see Day 41), Ch. XLVII.

204 Thomas Fuller, *Good Thoughts in Bad Times* (see Day 124), p. 132.

205 Maurice H. Harris, ed., *Hebraic Literature* (see Day 26), p. 4.

206 William Blake, *Jerusalem*. In *The Poetical Works of William Blake*, Oxford University Press, 1913, p. 410.

207 Monier Williams, ed., *Indian Wisdom* (see Day 3), pp. 147-149.

208 Proverbs 3:27-35, King James Version.

209 Y. P. Mei, trans., *The Works of Motse* (see Day 198), p. 155.

210 Matthew 25:31-36, 41-46, King James Version.

211 Lin Yutang, trans., *The Wisdom of China and India*. New York: Random House, 1942, p. 602.

212 Thomas S. Kepler, ed., *Letters and Reflections of François de Fénelon*. Cleveland and New York: World Publishing Co., 1955, pp. 126-127.

213 Edwin Collins, ed., *The Wisdom of Israel*. London: John Murray, 1910, p. 28.

214 James Legge, ed., *The Chinese Classics* (see Day 4), Part II, p. 201.

215 R. A. Nicholson, ed., *Rumi: Poet and Mystic* (see Day 50), p. 153.

216 F. Max Müller, ed., *The Sacred Books of the East*. Oxford: Clarendon Press, 1895, Vol. IV, pp. 35, 46-48.

217 Mark 12:28-34, King James Version.

218 W. H. D. Rouse, trans., *The Jataka* (see Day 67), Vol. II, Book III, Story 205, p. 105.

219 Raïssa Maritain, ed., *Léon Bloy, Pilgrim of the Absolute* (see Day 189), p. 218.

220 Edwin Collins, ed., *The Wisdom of Israel* (see Day 213), pp. 56-57.

221 Lin Yutang, ed., *The Wisdom of Laotse*. New York: Random House, 1948, pp. 145-146.

222 Arthur J. Arberry, trans., *The Koran Interpreted* (see Day 5), Vol. II, p. 335.

223 Psalm 46, King James Version.

224 M. N. Dhalla, *Zoroastrian Civilization*. London: Oxford University Press, 1922, p. 55; and F. Max Müller, ed., *The Sacred Books of the East*. Oxford: Clarendon Press, 1885, Vol. XXIII, p. 86.

225 Proverbs 25:11-14, Standard

American Edition of the Revised Version of the Bible (see Day 122).

226 C. G. Montefiore and H. Loewe, eds., *A Rabbinic Anthology* (see Day 144), p. 382.

227 E. Conze, ed., *Buddhist Texts Through the Ages* (see Day 2), p. 80.

228 John K. Ryan, ed. & trans., *Introduction to the Devout Life*, by St. Francis de Sales. New York: Harper & Row, 1950, pp. 180-181.

229 E. R. Hughes, ed., annotated and trans., *Chinese Philosophy in Classical Times*. Everyman's Library. New York: E. P. Dutton & Co., Inc., and London: J. M. Dent & Sons, Ltd., 1942, p. 221.

230 Monier Williams, ed., *Indian Wisdom* (see Day 3), pp. 147-149.

231 Psalm 95, King James Version.

232 Lin Yutang, ed., *The Wisdom of Laotse* (see Day 221), p. 312.

233 Luke 10:25-37, King James Version.

234 Adapted from F. L. Woodward, trans., *Some Sayings of the Buddha*. London: Oxford University Press, 1949, pp. 97-98.

235 R. A. Nicholson, ed., *Rumi: Poet and Mystic* (see Day 50), p. 55.

236 Psalm 96, King James Version.

237 Lin Yutang, ed., *The Wisdom of Confucius* (see Day 103), p. 104.

238 John K. Ryan, ed. & trans., *Introduction to the Devout Life*, by St. Francis de Sales (see Day 228), p. 54.

239 Lin Yutang, ed., *The Wisdom of Laotse* (see Day 221), pp. 134-135.

240 Luke 12:22-31, King James Version.

241 M. A. Macauliffe, ed., *The Sikh Religion* (see Day 88), Vol. I, pp. 79-80.

242 Monier Williams, ed., *Indian Wisdom* (see Day 3), p. 23.

243 C. G. Montefiore and H. Loewe, eds., *A Rabbinic Anthology* (see Day 144), p. 358.

244 Lin Yutang, ed., *The Wisdom of Confucius* (see Day 103), p. 186.

245 Psalm 103, King James Version.

246 Lionel Giles, ed., *The Sayings of Lao Tzu*. London: John Murray, 1905, p. 34.

247 F. L. Woodward, trans., *Some Sayings of the Buddha* (see Day 234), p. 90.

248 John K. Ryan, ed. & trans., *Introduction to the Devout Life*, by St. Francis de Sales (see Day 228), pp. 193-194.

249 Arthur J. Arberry, trans., *The Koran Interpreted* (see Day 5), Vol. II, p. 342.

250 Psalm 116, King James Version.

251 Lin Yutang, ed., *The Wisdom of Laotse* (see Day 221), p. 218.

252 S. Beal, ed., *Texts from the Buddhist Canon* (see Day 161), pp. 86-87.

253 C. G. Montefiore and H. Loewe, eds., *A Rabbinic Anthology* (see Day 144), p. 358.

254 Charles A. Wong, trans., *Books of Mencius*. China. (No publisher or date given), pp. 268-269.

255 Luke 18:9-14, King James Version.

256 Monier Williams, ed., *Indian Wisdom* (see Day 3), pp. 287-288.

257 C. W. Eliot, ed., *The Harvard Classics* (see Day 63), Vol. I, p. 346.

258 E. M. Hare, trans., *Woven Cadences of Early Buddhists* (see Day 116), pp. 74-75.

259 Lin Yutang, ed., *The Wisdom of China and India*. New York: Random House, 1942, pp. 769-770.

260 Psalm 127, King James Version.

261 Adapted from Lin Yutang, ed., *The Wisdom of China and India* (see Day 259), p. 587.

262 Luke 18:18-30, King James Version.

263 E. M. Hare, trans., *Woven Cadences of Early Buddhists* (*see* Day 116), pp. 16-19.

264 Monier Williams, ed., *Indian Wisdom* (*see* Day 3), pp. 281-

265 C. W. Eliot, ed., *The Harvard Classics* (*see* Day 63), Vol. I, pp. 376-377.

266 Lin Yutang, ed., *The Wisdom of Laotse* (*see* Day 221), p. 166.

267 Romans 12:9-21, King James Version.

268 Mrs. Rhys Davids, trans., *The Book of the Kindred Sayings* (*see* Day 107), Part I, pp. 276-278.

269 *Yoruba Poetry*, a special issue of *Black Orpheus*. Ibadan, Nigeria: General Publications Section, Ministry of Education, 1959.

270 Adapted from Charles Taylor, ed., *Sayings of the Jewish Fathers*. Cambridge: Cambridge University Press, 1897, pp. 29-32.

271 Monier Williams, ed., *Indian Wisdom* (*see* Day 3), pp. 445-446.

272 George Fox, *Journal*. New York: Everyman's Library, E. P. Dutton, 1924, pp. 6-7.

273 R. A. Nicholson, ed., *Rumi: Poet and Mystic* (*see* Day 50), p. 157.

274 I Corinthians 1:17-31, King James Version.

275 Monier Williams, ed., *Indian Wisdom* (*see* Day 3), p. 285.

276 Hu Shih, trans., in *Development of Logical Method in China*. Shanghai: The Oriental Book Co., 1922, p. 152.

277 Robert Bridges, ed., *Poems of Gerard Manley Hopkins*. London: Oxford University Press, 2nd ed., 1930, p. 26.

278 Adapted from Maurice H. Harris, ed., *Hebraic Literature* (*see* Day 26), p. 160.

279 Lin Yutang, ed., *The Wisdom of Laotse* (*see* Day 221), p. 164.

280 Monier Williams, ed., *Indian Wisdom* (*see* Day 3), pp. 442-443.

281 Adapted from John Burnet, ed., *Early Greek Philosophy*. London: A. & C. Black, Ltd., 1892, pp. 119-120.

282 I Corinthians 13, New English Bible. Oxford and Cambridge University Presses, 1961.

283 *Yoruba Poetry* (*see* Day 269).

284 Victor Gollancz, ed., *Man and God*. Boston: Houghton Mifflin, 1951, p. 342.

285 Monier Williams, ed., *Indian Wisdom* (*see* Day 3), pp. 515-516.

286 John Jeffrey, ed., *Moral and Religious Aphorisms*. Norwich, 1703, p. 170.

287 Lin Yutang, ed., *The Wisdom of Laotse* (*see* Day 221), p. 93.

288 Adapted from F. Max Müller, ed., *Ramakrishna*. New York: Charles Scribner's Sons, 1899, p. 122.

289 M. A. Macauliffe, ed., *The Sikh Religion* (*see* Day 88), Vol. I, pp. 71-72.

290 II Corinthians 6:1-18, King James Version.

291 Lin Yutang, ed., *The Wisdom of China and India*. New York: Random House, 1942, pp. 1063-1064.

292 Nicol Macnicol, trans., *Psalms of Maratha Saints*. Calcutta: Association Press, 1920, p. 69.

293 Lord Chalmers, trans., *Buddha's Teachings*. Cambridge: Harvard University Press, 1932, pp. 37-38.

294 Henry Vaughan, *The Mount of Olives: or, Solitary Devotions*. London, 1652. Reprinted in Henry Vaughan, *Poetry and Selected Prose*. London: Oxford University Press, 1963, p. 113.

295 Gregory the Great, *Morals on the Book of Job*, Vol. III. Oxford: John Henry Parker, 1844, p. 288.

296 T. Isaac Tambyah, trans., *Psalms of a Saiva Saint*. London: Luzac & Co., 1925, p. 3.

297 Galatians 6:1-10, King James Version.

235

298 E. R. Hughes, ed., annotated, and trans., *Chinese Philosophy in Classical Times* (see Day 229), pp. 19-20.

299 Victor Gollancz, ed., *Man and God* (see Day 284), p. 340.

300 John Donne: *Complete Poetry and Selected Prose*. London: The Nonesuch Press, 1929, pp. 321-322.

301 E. M. Hare, trans., *Woven Cadences of Early Buddhists* (see Day 116), pp. 93-94.

302 Monier Williams, ed., *Indian Wisdom* (see Day 3), pp. 445-446.

303 Lin Yutang, ed., *The Wisdom of Laotse* (see Day 221), p. 76.

304 F. Max Müller, ed., *The Sacred Books of the East* (see Day 216), Vol. IV, p. 383.

305 Ephesians 4:23-32, King James Version.

306 Francis Johnson, trans., *The Hitopadesa*, revised and in part rewritten by Lionel D. Barnett. Rewritten for this edition by William Robert Miller. London: Chapman and Hall, 1928, pp. 99, 100.

307 W. A. Wright, ed., *The Poetical Works of John Milton*. Cambridge: Cambridge University Press, 1903, p. 84.

308 Lin Yutang, ed., *The Wisdom of China and India* (see Day 259), p. 829.

309 Monier Williams, ed., *Indian Wisdom* (see Day 3), pp. 517-518.

310 II Thessalonians 3:10-15, King James Version.

311 Clement of Alexandria, The Stromata, IV, Ch. 23. *The Ante-Nicene Fathers*, Vol. II. Edinburgh, 1876.

312 Adapted from C. Kegan Paul, trans., *The Thoughts of Blaise Pascal*. London: George Bell & Sons, 1899, p. 93.

313 John S. Hoyland, ed., *An Indian Peasant Mystic*. London: Allenson & Co., Ltd., 1932, p. 50.

314 Lin Yutang, ed., *The Wisdom of Laotse* (see Day 221), p. 252.

315 James 1:22-27, King James Version.

316 Monier Williams, ed., *The Wisdom of India*. London: W. H. Allen, 1895, p. 449.

317 Matthew Arnold's translation quoted by John Baillie, *A Diary of Readings*. New York: Charles Scribner's Sons, 1955, p. 27.

318 Ch'u Ta-Kao, trans., *Tao-Te-Ching* (see Day 41), Ch. XLI.

319 Adapted from *Menog-i-Khrad* 2, 98-108 in *The Sacred Books of the East*, ed., F. Max Müller, Oxford: Clarendon Press, 1885, Vol. XXIV, p. 16.

320 James 2:5b-10, King James Version.

321 F. Max Müller, ed., *The Sacred Books of the East*. Oxford: Clarendon Press, 1886, Vol. XXV, pp. 155-156.

322 William Law, *A Serious Call to a Devout and Holy Life*. London: J. M. Dent & Sons, 1906, pp. 197-198.

323 Ch'u ta-Kao, trans., *Tao-Te-Ching* (see Day 41), Ch. LXXVI.

324 Benjamin Jowett, trans., *The Dialogues of Plato* (see Day 174), Vol. I, pp. 422-423.

325 James 2:14-26, King James Version.

326 Y. P. Mei, trans., *The Works of Motse* (see Day 198), p. 136.

327 *The Practice of the Presence of God: Letters and Conversations of Brother Lawrence*, Eng. trans. London, 1892.

328 Monier Williams, ed., *Indian Wisdom* (see Day 3), p. 443.

329 Paraphrase by William Robert Miller for this edition, based on M. A. Macauliffe, ed., *The Sikh Religion* (see Day 88), Vol. 4, p. 260.

330 I John 3:9-11, 14-16, King James Version.

331 Monier Williams, ed., *Indian Wisdom* (see Day 3), p. 444.

332 John Donne, quoted in E. A. Blackburn, *A Treasury of the Kingdom*. New York: Oxford

University Press, 1954, p. 273.
333 C. G. Montefiore and H. Loewe, eds., *A Rabbinic Anthology* (*see* Day 144), p. 103.
334 Ch'u Ta-Kao, trans., *Tao-Te-Ching* (*see* Day 41), Ch. XXVII.
335 Adapted from John Donne, *Complete Poetry and Selected Prose,* edited by John Hayward. London: The Nonesuch Press, 1941, pp. 357-359.
336 Monier Williams, ed., *Indian Wisdom* (*see* Day 3), pp. 445-446.
337 John Jeffrey, ed., *Moral and Religious Aphorisms* (*see* Day 286), pp. 70, 88, 102.
338 *Yoruba Poetry* (*see* Day 269).
339 Fyodor Dostoevsky, *The Brothers Karamazov,* trans. by David Magarshack. Harmondsworth: Penguin Books, Ltd., 1958.
340 M. A. Macauliffe, *The Sikh Religion* (*see* Day 88), Vol. I, p. 116.
341 Adapted from Susanna Winkworth, trans., "Sermon on the 4th Sunday in Lent," *The History and Life of the Reverend Doctor John Tauler of Strasbourg With Twenty-Five of His Sermons.* New York: Wiley and Halsted, 1858.
342 Y. P. Mei, trans., *The Works of Motse* (*see* Day 198), p. 139.
343 John S. Hoyland, ed., *An Indian Peasant Mystic* (*see* Day 313), pp. 78, 79.
344 C. G. Montefiore and H. Loewe, eds., *A Rabbinic Anthology* (*see* Day 144), p. 257.
345 M. N. Dutt, trans., *Srimad Bhagavatam.* Calcutta: Elysium Press, 1896, Sec. 7:64-65.
346 A. Jeremias, trans., Akkadian Counsels of Wisdom, in James Hastings, ed., *Encyclopedia of Religion and Ethics.* New York: Charles Scribner's Sons, 1908, Vol. III, p. 747.
347 Martin Buber, *Tales of the Hasidim, the Early Masters,* trans. by Olga Marx. New York:

Schocken Books, 1947, pp. 71, 74, 51.
348 John Jeffrey, ed., *Moral and Religious Aphorisms* (*see* Day 286), pp. 102, 112, 20, 12.
349 Swami Prabhavananda and Christopher Isherwood, trans., *The Song of God: Bhagavad-Gita.* New York: New American Library, 1954, p. 98.
350 Ebrahim Khan, ed., *Anecdotes from Islam.* Lahore: Muhammad Ashraf, 1947, p. 152.
351 John Clark Archer, ed., *The Sikhs* (*see* Day 114), p. 124.
352 Adapted from Monier Williams, ed., *Indian Wisdom* (*see* Day 3), pp. 46-47.
353 Paraphrase by William Robert Miller, from Susanna Winkworth, trans., *The History and Life of . . . Dr. John Tauler* (*see* Day 341).
354 Monier Williams, ed., *Indian Wisdom* (*see* Day 3), p. 444.
355 Psalm 130, King James Version.
356 F. Max Müller, ed., *The Sacred Books of the East* (*see* Day 216), Vol. IV, pp, 22-24.
357 Nicol Macnicol, trans., *Psalms of Maratha Saints* (*see* Day 292), pp. 68-69.
358 R. A. Nicholson, ed., *Rumi: Poet and Mystic* (*see* Day 50), p. 98.
359 M. A. Macauliffe, *The Sikh Religion* (*see* Day 88), Vol. 4, pp. 259-260.
360 Monier Williams, ed., *Indian Wisdom* (*see* Day 3), p. 448.
361 E. M. Hare, trans., *Woven Cadences of Early Buddhists* (*see* Day 116), pp. 12-13.
362 E. R. Hughes, ed., annotated, and trans., *Chinese Philosophy in Classical Times* (*see* Day 229), pp. 39-40.
363 Victor Gollancz, ed., *Man and God* (*see* Day 284), p. 342.
364 Swami Prabhavananda and Christopher Isherwood, trans., *The Song of God: Bhagavad-Gita* (*see* Day 349), pp. 84-85.
365 Ch'u Ta-Kao, trans., *Tao-Te-Ching* (*see* Day 41), Ch. XXIV.